Business Dining Etiquette Guide 101   Harold Almon's

Business Dining Etiquette Guide 101   In US
Professional and Graduate   ISBN 978-0-917921-48-3
Job Preparation Four Pack

Interview Dining Etiquette
Eating in Style

University Etiquette
Outclass the Competition

An At Ease Press Etiquette Guide
A Be at Ease School of Etiquette Course Guide

(151)

Text by
Harold Almon

Published by
At Ease Press schoolofetiquette@ateasepress.com

Business Dining Etiquette Guide 101

ISBN 978-0-917921-48-3
Copyright (c) 2016, 2017
Printed in the United States of America

Text by
Harold Almon

To: Proofreaders and reviewers;

If you have additions, corrections, or questions let me know, the worst it can get you is an updated copy

Your forever rewriter

Acknowledgements

To Miss Ann (Mom),

Thank you for taking me to see the signals.

The bolded items are included in a PowerPoint Presentation.

Foreword

Business Dining Etiquette Guide 101 Job Preparation Four Pack Interview Dining Etiquette is Book I of a set.

Book I provides an excellent opportunity to learn (or brush up on) Table Manners, Rules of Etiquette used While Eating, Pre Steps, Presents, Something to Drink, USA Menu Number and Order of Courses, Setting a Place Setting for One, Using a Napkin, Eating Bread and Butter, Using Glasses at Table, Spoon Rules, Rest Positions, Using Cutlery, Eating in Style American and Continental, Salt Rules, How to Eat Chicken Bone-in with a Knife and Fork, and Saying Thank You.

Dining is a ritual at which more than eating is done. What you eat is up to you. How you eat is your present to the table, and the view you provide to those around you. The way a person eats reflects on that person and on his or her company. But above all that , when sitting at a table and sharing a meal with a friend it is wonderful to know what is being signaled and what to signal back. Look educated best. Get etiquette, and outclass the competition. Practice can be done in casual shoes.

Table Manners

Table manners are "Rules (of etiquette) used while eating." –
Wikipedia. Look educated best.

1.   The way you dine can add to someone's acceptance of you. In
      offering food, someone may be offering you a piece of
      himself or herself or an allegiance. Someone could be saying,
      "Thank you" and/or might be evaluating you: to see from
      where you have come, and how far it is to where you need to
      be, and to see if eating with you again is something to want to
      do. Eat to please your host and hostess where possible, and to
      please yourself within reason.

2.   Your presence is an affirmation that you understand that
      more than eating is being done.

3.   In business, on the policy making level, you know that your
      ascension has begun when someone says to you (more than
      once), "Let's do lunch."

4.   Eat, by not eating, you can cause yourself to be watched. For
      refusing food, you may be called everything from, "A stick in
      the mud," to "Downright inhospitable." You could cause your
      decision to be interpreted as an insult to the culinary skills of
      the person who offered the food. This person might think that
      more than food is being refused. Reject food and you become
      subject to the question, (spoken or unspoken,) "My food not
      good enough for you?" You cannot make the person who
      offered the foods understand.

5. Join student organizations. There is usually food at each meeting. Attend business luncheons and functions. Do it for exposure, publicity, and to scout out where may be a neat place to eat when the function requires reciprocity.

6. **Pre-steps:** RSVP, accept "the "kind" invitation. Respond to invitations within twenty-four hours to one week of receipt. Avoid being a No show if possible. Few want to stare at your empty chair.

7. Identify meal restrictions. Alert your host or hostess as to any meal restrictions along with your acceptance of an invitation. Review the on-line menu. Decide what item in the mid-price point you want to order. Practice eating cocktail food. Practice eating food that is difficult to eat, before the meeting. **Eat a little something before you get there.** In home training, remember, "Do not eat that now. You will spoil your dinner." In public life, it can quickly change to, "Eat a little something after leaving home." "Do not make them think that I never give you money or feed you." Before a meal where you are to be a guest and will be looked upon is the time to use that two for one fast food coupon.

8. Meet the dress request. Dress as your host expects. Dress professionally. Avoid directly pointing out or correcting the dining behavior of anyone not considered family. For a family member you can get a copy of this book (or the one I just updated.

Dining Stations and Line

Dining Stations and Lines

■ Station One	- The Meeting Line	The Line to Presents
■ Station Two	- The Reception Line -	NA
■ Station Three	- The Bar -	Something to Drink
■ Station Four	- The Table - Menu Number / Order of Courses	
■		A Place Setting for One A Cover
Station Five	- The Food	- The Order of Service
■ Station Six	- The Bathroom	NA
■ Station Seven	- The Line "To Go"	Things to Take Away
Station Eight	- Line to Good-bye	– Saying Thank You
-Correspondence Cards Stamps		Acceptance & Regret

Be at Ease School of Etiquette in Austin -
baeaee.com

9. **The meeting line: Find out the** name location and time of the meeting. Engine search the location and map directions.

10. **Be punctual. Arrive, "Just in time,"** whatever this means in your community. You can get there early and take a walk around the block. You can wait in the downstairs lobby. You may visit a restroom to tidy up. Avoid showing up early in the reception area.

11. **The Reception Line The line to Presents: socially, occasionally show up with a present, where appropriate.**

Job Interview Tips: Presents for an interview:

Remember the purpose of the meal
Adhere to the dress request.
Brings copies of your resume or ready one for forwarding.
Have a pen and note pad.
Research the company. Complete a company fact sheet.
Practice responses to interview questions.
Prepare a list of questions to ask.
Follow the lead of your host or hostess.
Eat something before you get there.

Look educated best. Get University Etiquette. Outclass the Competition.

The Line to the Bar

Practice getting something to drink, introductions and handshaking. Something to drink can be a club soda with a twist, or a fruit juice. Few want to pay for your pretentious water.

Something to drink is to be given in a glass with a cocktail napkin. OK then, ask for, or go get one. When standing, **the cocktail napkin** is to be picked up and placed on your left hand between the middle and ring finger. It **can be held between the index and middle fingers.**

Drink, when a sip is desired

1. **The glass is to be lifted by the stem by the right hand thumb, and index and middle fingers of the right hand.** A glass can be lifted by the bowl, when it contains red wine. It may be lifted at the base, just because. **The elbow is to be kept down and in, moved forward; and wrist to hand stem moved upward, a sip (pour) of the beverage is to be taken** into the mouth directly from the edge of the glass.

   Avoid the crane: lifting your elbow up, so high it could poke someone in the eye, in order to take a drink from a glass (Hee Haw).

2.   **The cocktail straw** provided with a drink is called a stirrer. It **is to be used as such: only for stirring**. It can be used, but then is to be discarded. It can be removed and held under the glass. It may be held to the side of the glass between the index and middle fingers. It is hard to "Mac" (look cool) sipping a drink from a stirrer.

3.   While drinking, you can avoid slurping or guzzling by closing your upper lip between any liquid and the edge of any glass, and then pouring the liquid into your mouth. You may avoid chewing a beverage by simply swallowing small amounts of it. Leave a little of each beverage in each glass.

4.   When a pre-dinner drink is rested it can be carried on the palm of the left hand, held by the thumb and the index finger. The right hand is to be kept warm, free, and dry as much as possible.

5.   When it is finished, it is to be placed back on the palm of the left hand, or on a bar, or table atop a cocktail napkin used as coaster in the place setting position in which it was set.

Overcoming Coffee Shop Behaviors & Café Ways

When ordering in a coffee Shop or café get a cup "for here:"
One is usually available with a saucer, for the asking; Ok, get a
mug, even a mug alone has so much more cache than a cardboard
glass and a sleeve, Styrofoam glass, or a metal container with a lid
on it: an adult Sippy-cup.

A napkin is to be provided when you are drinking anything. OK go
get one. The corner of a napkin is to be used to gently blot the
mouth before taking a sip of any beverage while eating.

1. A spoon can be used to stir sugar, milk, or cream placed in a
    mug or coffee cup. **Sugar is to be in cubes (and served with
    tongs.) When packets are present use no more than two.**
    Leave the empty packets to the left of your saucer.

    When passed or finished, the spoon is to be placed on the
    right side of the cup atop a saucer. The spoon used for a mug
    is left in the place where the drink was dressed.

    A coffee mug or teacup is to be held by pinching the handle
    between the thumb and the index finger. It can be held **with
    the index finger though the handle, the thumb placed
    above it, and the middle finger placed below**. The cup is to
    be picked up by the handle with the right hand and taken to
    the mouth to take a drink (pour) from it. (The right elbow is
    to remain down and in, handle for a reason.)

2.   An espresso for here is to come in a ceramic demitasse cup set atop a demitasse saucer. To the rest of the world, this is a coffee. The cup is to be held by pinching the handle between the thumb and the index finger of the right hand.

3.   When drinking from a cup (or glass), **avoid sticking your little finger out** at a ninety-degree angle when you lift the vessel to your mouth, unless you really do have arthritis. Be natural. Be yourself.

4.   The resting position for a saucer is directly atop a table. **The rest and finished position for a cup is atop a saucer handle to four o'clock.** When seated, the rest position for a mug is directly on the table handle at four o'clock. It is one of three non-plates that can be placed upon a table without an underlying plate. Occasionally, for practice; get a cup "for here." Under a roof, avoid spending your whole life drinking from a lid covered glass or container, or sucking liquids from one with a straw.

Ask for a ceramic plate, if you get something to eat. The view you provide for someone else is worth the tax- if any. Each may now justify you putting a tip in that jar in clear view. For this you could carry cash. At some places tips cannot be added to credit card tabs, but may be added when using a wireless application. Short of using a plate, in the Continental style, food has been seen eaten from atop a bag; it can serve as a plate. In the America style food has been seen being eaten from inside a bag; it is a coffee shop habit without the same grace.

Plan on how to provide or exchange contact information. Wait until it or a card is offered by the senior person.

Always accept contact information; it provides a way to say thank you. Have a card to return in kind. When you are "temporarily out" you can provide email contact information. It may also be part of an email signature configuration.

Before you give your contact information, update your email address signature, and your link to your on line profiles. Ensure each is appropriate for the recipient.

You may attach a resume to an email ready for forwarding to a contact, or to a new acquaintance.

You could get a number, from an acquaintance, call that person, or have that person call you, and then establish that person as a contact. This is the new old school.

When you can get a wireless application that can be used to exchange contact information, do so.

Getting Cards

Get business cards. **Ask, "Do you have a card?"** When you get a card, take time to look at it: as if to give approval, say something nice when you can. Say, "Please" and "Thank you" as needed.

Using Small Plates

At a business party

1. A small plate, usually a bread and butter plate, can be held on the index finger of the left hand and secured by the thumb. It may also be rested on the side of the middle finger. It could then be used to hold cocktail food. You might use a bread and butter plate as an underlying plate for a bowl.

2. A salad/dessert plate could held in the same manner, and used for the same thing. This can be harder to do especially without, muscle memory, practice. You can pack a salad plate in a zip locking bag and use it as a plate to hold food provided in a serving container. You may use the salad/dessert plate as an under lying plate for a bowl. Avoid refilling a used plate from a buffet table, setting a used plate on a buffet table, and from stacking plates at any table. Avoid taking cocktail food or drink out of the area in which it was served.

3. A salad bowl when used to serve salad could be used without an underlying plate, as the second of three non-plate items that may be used with this rule. Even a finger bowl when set in a place setting is to be set upon a doily.

    If you are served part of a meal in a bowl without an underlying plate, and it is not being used to hold a salad, be careful what you get for dessert; as a treat, you might be given a biscuit.

The Line to Table Talk Invocation and Conversation

The First Seat Seat of Honor at Table

The first seat to be   assigned at a table is the
seat of honor As a rule of thumb this seat is
given to the host (HT) He can relinquish it for
a head of state or a date A host /hostess or
escort is to be assigned to   each table

Be at Ease School of Etiquette in Austin -
beease.com

Before you sit, wait until, the host or the senior person at table has taken a seat. Conversation at a table is to begin immediately after people are seated.

You can do a self-introduction by saying first to the person on your right and then to your left, "I am ...," followed by your first and last name. You can show your name place card and say, "My name." A woman may reply to an introduction by saying "I am...," followed by her first and last name if she is single. If she is married or considerably older than you she could say, "I am, So and so's wife." Providing her husband's first and last name.

At a family meal, or an official meal, an invocation may interrupt conversation. A host is responsible for the invocation. This duty can be delegated to and performed by any person in the assembly. When this person is you, **know an invocation acceptable to your host's culture.** Say something "Impromptu" or a standard such as

1. "For what we are about to receive, Lord, make us truly grateful, Amen." (All or Christian)

2. "God be at our table." (All)

3. "O Lord, forgive us our sins and bless these gifts in Jesus' name, Amen. (Christian)

4. "Bless us, O Lord, and these thy gifts which we are about to receive from thy bounty through Christ our Lord, Amen." (Catholic)

An invocation may be any in which everyone feels comfortable in you saying. An invocation can be said at a banquet.

An invocation is to be omitted at a business meeting and at a dinner party in a private home. It is the etiquette. You can ask if one is desired, explain the rule, or omit it.

A personal prayer "Let the table conversation stay at the same decibel level as the invocation."

The difference in a cafeteria, café, or a coffee shop and a formal casual and fine dining room anywhere is the decibel level of the conversations in them.   Speak with your inside (soft) voice. Nothing as sweet as being able to hear yourself as you eat.

A host is responsible for controlling dinner conversation at table: volume and tone. It is to be civil, tranquil, and social, even among families.

Talk quietly to the people in the room; talk to people on your cellular telephone in another room. For now, turn off your cellular telephone or set it to vibrate. For dining partners, conversation can be about school, majors, parents, children, vacations, trips, and people in the news and/or about current happenings. **Talk. Some food can be in your mouth just not seen. Make agreeable talk with your dinner partner(s.) Your voice is to be modulated and** well-paced. Conversation is spearheaded by asking a question about the person with whom you are talking or by revealing a fact about yourself then asking a follow up question. Be intent in hearing the views of those around you. Continue conversation in this fashion. Conversation is to be of wit that is quick and of humor that is kind. Table talk is to contain only information that can be passed. It is an unspoken rule; private conversation is to be conducted in private. Pretend that a microphone is just under the table and that it is open.

Avoid table talk about religion, age, salary, marriage, table manners, or etiquette. Conversation may be changed by someone saying, in a slightly louder voice, "How about those Yankees."

At a formal meal, conversation is always a series of two by two conversations. First, information is to be passed to the woman on your right. The same or updated information can be passed to the woman on your left with the change of the course. This action is called "Turning the table." Informally, dinner conversation may be briefly switched across or down the table.

At the next turn your partner can relay any new information. With enough courses most of what you said will get back to you. At a social meal, avoid talking "Shop" at mealtime unless to do so is the expressed purpose. Do this by saying, "I would be glad to get that information to you. Could you call my office tomorrow?"

At a business meal, allow the host or hostess to initiate the business conversation, unless there is a failure to do so, and a significant amount of time has passed. Business talk is to begin at breakfast right after receiving coffee, and at lunch right after the food-order has been taken. The business lunch; takes place because some has something to sell promote or discuss. If the talk is to be serious, one can order one drink at the table and then order lunch promptly. **At a business dinner, business talk can begin after dessert is ordered but before it arrives. Avoid props when you can. At a, "Getting to know you/joint spouse dinner" business talk may be omitted altogether.**

Job Interview tip:

Complete a company fact sheet/review.

At a job interview, you could be asked, "What do you know about the company." And good for you, you know a thing or two. Your resume can be re-done to reflect that you have looked at the job description, and that you are ready for this discussion. You may have new resumes ready for presentation, or for forwarding by attachment electronically.

The Standard USA Menu Number of Courses

USA Menu – Number and Order of Courses

The standard United States of America menu, no matter how formal, consists of no more than five (four) courses. You can check with the White House. Practice eating in courses over eating in piles.

The first course could be an appetizer. It might precede or substitute as a first course. As a rule the first course is to be soup. It can be fruit-juice or melon. The first course may be omitted. Avoid serving rolls or sliced bread and butter or Olive oil, or chips and dips, as an intended first course.

The second course can be a fish, with maybe a potato item, or at lunch, it may be an egg dish. This course could be omitted.

The third or main course (sometimes called the entrée in restaurants) is to be a roasted meat (a Roti,) a fowl, or a vegetable item, and two vegetable side items, (or informally one side item may be a starch item.)

At least one non-meat main course item is to be included in each group of menu selections offered.

The fourth course might be a green salad **with cheese.** *
Salad served before a main course stems from what I call a
Mickey D's mentality: greet a guest within 30 seconds; give
each something to drink within three minutes, and
something to eat within seven.

C'est tres gourmet - not really. The drink before you eat is an
aperitif and something to eat before a main course can be a
consommé. The purpose of a salad is to push the main course
away. This course may be served in lieu of a third course. It may
be omitted in favor of dessert.

The fifth or last course is to be dessert. Coffee can be served
with dessert, after it, or omitted entirely.

Where allowed and appropriate, to each dessert you can add or
have added cookies **bought during a fund raiser such as**
chocolate cookies with pink M & Ms in them made and
purchased in support of the cure for breast cancer (Thanks
Melissa.)

You may add a few chocolate covered mint cookies, or
chocolate stripped coconut cookies, acquired in support of a
Scout or as part of Giving Back.

What is served in each course may change with personal
preference and pallet of each Chef. In the United States of
America this is the standard menu frame.

A trend has developed of omitting the first and second course. Most meals consist of a fourth and a third course: a salad and a main course. The latter practice is seen often in commercial dining rooms. There a dessert is seen and had only by the very lucky.

If you are going to share a meal with someone, eat in courses over eating in piles. At minimum, plan on a two-part lunch: a first course and a main course, or a main course and a dessert. It takes a little extra time, allows for longer conversation, and builds in great memories.

Plan a three-course dinner: a first course, main course, and a dessert. At a public meal, you can offer to share a dessert. At a business meal, omit doing this.

Review the menu at each place to which you will take someone. And if you wish, know the signature dish not to be missed. If you are invited to share a meal with someone, eat a little something before you leave home.

Ah yes, and learn the most favorable parking instructions. See if the parking pass for your guest can be validated by the restaurant. The discount for the special of the day can be overshadowed by the cost of the valet.

At a table
the first thing done
is not a prayer
but to discover

A Place Setting for One
Called -- A Cover

Rules for Setting a Place Setting for One – A Cover

A place setting for one person at a table is called a cover; it is contained in an area fifteen inches up from the table edge and twelve inches on each side from center each person. **Items in a place setting are to be placed based on a likely menu: which courses will be served and when.**

"A cover is a road map for a meal." Maintain your cover or establish one. The spoon for coffee may be omitted from the place setting, except maybe at breakfast; here coffee can be served with or before the first course. A stem less glass is to be used for breakfast. I overlook this rule of etiquette as often as I can.

A Place Setting Deconstructed

Maintaining your cover or establishing one.

1. A folded napkin, six letters (C-E-N-T-E-R,) is to be placed center a place setting or plate in absence of a first course. **For special occasions it can be seventeen to twenty-two inches square fabric napkin folded in a signature fold.** Informally the square napkin can be made of paper. A folded napkin can be placed to the left of the forks when a first course is to be in place. It is to be untouched by the fork(s.)(I do not know where the practice of placing a fork atop a napkin got started; perhaps in a café when table sanitation was suspect or outside where there was a lot of wind.)

    A course - also six letters can be preset center a place setting. It may be omitted and be brought in to the table.

2. Flatware is to be placed approximately one inch up from the edge of the table or placemat evenly spaced and in symmetry.

    The fork, four letters (L-E-F-T,) is to be placed to the left of the plate space. It can be placed tines up or tines down. The place (or meat) knife, five letters (R-I-G-H-T,) is to be placed to the right of the plate space blade facing toward the center. A place knife is to accompany a place fork for all meals except a buffet meal. It can be placed for one as for all other meals. It may be placed next to the fork to the right for a buffet meal.

3.   The water glass, five letters, (R-I-G-H-T,) is to be set in place
     above the right tip of the knife. Yes, that is your glass for
     water.

     A water glass is to be set in cover whenever entertaining
     company. (Now, you can add another diagonally to the right
     of it for whatever goes into your glass for "wine.")

Each spoon is to be placed to the right of the last knife bowl up or
down to match the fork(s.) (The rule has always been, "Go from
the outside in - in kind." In kind: all knives then all spoons.

When the table is correctly set, first all the knives are set, then the
number 1 spoon, placed to the right of the last knife, set bowl-up
or bowl-down to match the fork(s,) you get the idea. The number
2 spoon, if required for dessert can be set above the plate, handle to
the right, and the number 3 spoon for coffee can be omitted from
the setting.

At a table, a plate is to be set center the place setting one inch up
from the edge of it. Avoid wrapping your arm around it, or holding
it on the tips of your fingers; (both these things I have seen.)

Next to each place setting you may place a piece of signature candy. In public, when appropriate, you could get the candy (from the counter) on the way in.

A party favor: a small (return) gift or party loot bag given to inspire the remembrance of an event – (especially a dinner party,) or as a gesture of thanks for a gift or attendance could be placed next to each place setting.

At a table, practice, avoid making personal items: bags, backpacks, books, or technology part of a cover. Each can be placed on a lap, chair. Technology that cannot be placed in a chair may be kept on the floor or in a pocket. You can say, "Excuse me," and step away from the table to take a vibrating telephone call.

Allow the senior woman to pick up flatware first. This is a universal indicator; others are, to "Dig in."

Napkin Rules

A napkin is to be used to signal when eating is to begin. After the invocation or after someone says, "Please enjoy your dinner." **A napkin is to be picked up at the lead of the hostess or senior person at the table.** This is the indicator that others at table are to do so. A napkin is not to stay on the table. Even at a dinner for two.

1. **When seated at a table, a napkin is to be picked up, folded in half, and placed or replaced on your lap fold towards you prior to eating or drinking anything.** It can be placed on your lap quartered for breakfast and for Continental or fast food. It may be placed in half or in a three quarter fold the long way for dinner size napkins: twenty-two to seventeen inches, or entirely opened for lunch size napkins: fifteen inches or less. Any fold is to be towards you.

2. After several people have been served guests are to begin eating. **One corner of the napkin is to be used to correct conditions at table disturbed by the act of eating**. Gently rub the tips of your fingers against the corner of one to remove foodstuffs collected during the course of eating. This corner could be folded under before using it again.

3. The courtesy of napkin use is asked: to keep your grease off the glass, and to give your food time to pass. One corner of the napkin can be used to blot the mouth gently prior to taking a sip (pour) of any beverage.

4. A napkin is to remain on your lap as long as you continue to eat or to drink at a table. When leaving a table temporarily, your napkin is to be placed on your chair (to indicate your pending return.) (For this some bring to table a bag or a book.)

5. In a commercial dining room, a napkin can be placed on your chair, when you stand to greet a person who has stopped to visit your table. It may be kept there until a senior man asks you to, "Please, be seated," or until a woman leaves. In a commercial dining room, you could omit standing when you are visited by a man or woman who is working there, unless the person is also a close friend.

6. In a private home, a napkin that is dropped is to be retrieved and continued in use. Nonchalantly, get it back. When a napkin is dropped on the floor in a commercial dining room, it is time for a replacement. It is to be left on the floor. The host is to let the server know that a new one is now required. It may be retrieved, but it is no longer to be used above the table. Go ahead, and get a new one.

7. At the end of a meal, at the lead of the hostess or the senior person, the napkin is to be placed in a mock fold to the left **(leaving side)** of your place setting: indicating that you are done and leaving. **The rule: a napkin is not to end on a plate.**

A napkin can be placed into a ring and set to the right (remaining side) of your place setting at home: indicating that you are done and will be attending the next meal. The fact that your napkin ring is distinctive from all others ensures you will get the same napkin at the next feeding.

A napkin, even a paper one, is to be treated such that at the conclusion of a meal it looks within reason as it did at the beginning, even when it is made of paper. The person closest to doing this wins "the napkin game." **The secret is to use only one corner of it. You are only to get one**. Avoid the urge to use your napkin to blow or to wipe your nose at a table. To do this, excuse yourself from the table and use a handkerchief; ok for some of you that may mean use some bathroom tissue.

8. In the United States of America the napkin has been seen used to surrender a place setting; lifted up, waded, and tossed center the plate as if to say, "See I am done." It can sometimes be seen opened up, and spread out over a plate as a sign of, "Dead plate." These are practices from people who do not often get to use fabric napkins and from which I hope you are now rescued.

Everyone invited to a table deserves a better fate than expecting a napkin and being given a paper towel. But the hostess needs to know that you know the rules for handling a fabric one.

A napkin can be tucked in at the neck by you or any person eating a full lobster dinner and/or when you are sitting next to anyone else who is trying to, especially when lobster bibs have been omitted. It may be placed in at the neck of anyone eating on an airplane whenever they want. If you're wearing a tie, this beats throwing the tips over your shoulder. At all other times a napkin is to be placed on a lap.

A napkin can be used to pick up a piece of chicken or meat you dropped on your host's floor. Yes, if a replacement piece is not offered you can eat the one dropped, (but only at a host's home.) You can starve anywhere.

In a commercial dining room, a napkin is used to cover something that dropped on a floor, leave both there. Ask the host for a new napkin. He will call a service person. The server can use the napkin to lift up whatever it was that was dropped. When you are the host, tip this person as if you are grateful.

The napkin may be used by a server to fold it into a fancy fold to present you with mints and your check. If no other creative service was preformed, you might provide your usual tip.

In fast food service, everyone deserves a minimum, a napkin. It can be used to practice for when you give a dinner party, and to distinguish its use from a paper towel.

A napkin may be used to crumb a table and to hold under a plate held in the left hand on the way to the trash can. Even a paper napkin deserves a better fate than being stuffed into a glass.

Water at Table

When a guest is to be at table a water glass is to be set at each setting. When under a roof "Water for here" is to be served in a glass. The water glass is to be set to the right of the plate space above the tip of the knife. Yes, this is your glass. In a private home, each water goblet is to be filled ¾ full prior to the time people come to the table.

In a commercial dining room, water is to be served, after people are seated, from the right. When a beverage is to be served in addition to water, a water glass can be used for it or a glass specifically named for the beverage to be served may be added to the right of it.

In informal service, water can be provided when requested and given in a ceramic glass or a cup. Avoid asking for and or using a lid or a straw. At some point, omit the Sippy cup and risk that the drink might not tip.

Before taking a drink of any beverage eating implements are to be placed in the rest position for the style in which you are eating. Pat or blot your mouth with the corner of your napkin and return it to your lap.

A water glass is to be picked up by the stem with the right hand, and with elbow down and in, taken to the mouth, and a sip (pour) of water is to be taken.

The rest and finished position for the glass is in the table setting position. At a table, avoid placing a napkin under a water glass.

In a private home, the water glass can be refilled at the table, by a server, or guests from a pitcher on the table, or the hostess can offer it from a pitcher on a sideboard.

In a commercial dining room, the water glass can be refilled by a server without being lifted from the table.

Using Glasses at Table

A pre-dinner drink can be offered at a table when one was omitted at a bar. It is called an aperitif: (an appetite starter.) It is to be placed to the right of all other glasses. In a commercial dining room, a pre-dinner drink is to be placed atop a cocktail napkin when it is served, rested, or finished. It and this glass may be removed when the drink is finished.

When seated at a dining table a large napkin is to be placed on your lap fold towards you, before drinking or eating anything.

A guest may be heard to say, "Please order me a drink. I'll be right back," or "Where can I wash my hands." A guest could wait to do this until after reading or ordering from a reusable menu. Once someone does this, expect the next act: a visit to the bathroom; it is station six. Now remember, put your napkin on your chair seat, on a book or a bag on your chair if you like, and "Go wash your hands and get ready to come to or stay at the table."

Avoid keeping a dinner napkin as part of your cover. When you are in a chair at a table, it is to be atop of your lap.

Which Drinks' Mine

It is my wish to assist you in locating the drink which is yours and knowing which drink is mine.

1. "With each hand make an OK sign.
2. Place each hand on the table.
3. Left to right – where you see the "b" is the side for your bread. Where you see "d" is the side for your drink."
4. To the subject say, "Good night." That glass to your right is yours. This one is mine.

Avoid making the OK sign in public at other times. In some cultures it is the same as making the finger.

Avoid adding a straw or lid to any glass "For here" to be used inside. Straws can be used in a container or can, anywhere, inside you can remove the lid. Remember the sign; beverages are to be taken up from the right side using the right hand.

To Take a Drink

When at table, place your eating implements in the rest position for style in which you are eating. Pat the napkin to your lips and place it back on your lap. Then, with elbows down and in, take a drink.

Avoid being at table drink in one hand and napkin or food in the other.

A Bread and Butter Plate

A bread and butter plate is to be placed above the tines of the place fork. It can be placed to the left of the last fork, with the top in approximate line with the plate space or tines of the place fork. It may be placed one inch up from the edge of a round table.

A butter spreader can be placed horizontally across the top back of a bread and butter plate, handle pointed to the right, blade facing the edge of the table. It may be placed diagonally with the handle pointed to three-o'clock. It could be placed to the right of this plate, in a vertical position parallel with the place fork.

Note: the use of this plate is optional. It can be omitted from a truly formal place setting where butter is omitted; the roll, biscuit, or bread item may be laid directly on the tablecloth unbuttered.

Bread can be placed center a place setting underneath a folded napkin. It may be placed on a bread and butter plate.

At an informal meal the bread item could be pre-buttered and placed directly on the tablecloth or placemat. Note: bread is not a first course.

Eating Bread and Butter

Bread is not a first course. A biscuit, bun, muffin, or roll is to be eaten with a main course. Avoid eating bread and butter (or olive oil) as a first course. Bread can be provided as atmosphere, but is to be eaten after the main course is placed in front of you. In a commercial dining room, if you would like an appetizer or a first course, order one.

Bread may be served in a tray or basket before or almost as soon as you are seated at table. Bread is to be placed on a bread and butter plate. It can be placed onto the side of a dinner plate using a pair of tongs. Each person could be required to take bread using his or her fingers. Bread can be pre-set at each place setting on a bread and butter (B&B) plate, or more formally on a plate underneath a fancy folded napkin. It may be preset unbuttered on a tablecloth.

Untoasted bread, cold or hot, that is about to be eaten is to be broken apart/detached from a larger piece with the fingers as needed.

Avoid ever cutting a roll with a knife. Bread can be placed on a bread and butter plate and buttered. A butter spreader (or meat knife) is to be used to spread butter onto bread. The rest position for the butter spreader is diagonally across the top of the B&B plate, blade facing toward the edge of the table, and handle pointed to four o'clock. Then this small piece is placed in the mouth using your right hand. Repeat, bread is to be eaten, knife at rest, with the right hand. Avoid using bread as a test instrument to see which teeth are intact: showing teeth marks in bread you are eating.

Small biscuits can be eaten without being broken. Rolls and muffins may be broken in half or in small pieces as needed, never larger than one bite at a time. **Butter each bite at a time.** A butter spreader (or a meat knife) is to be used to spread butter, jam, jelly, and cream cheese onto bread. A torn off piece of bread can be held on the B&B plate, and dressed prior to being eaten. Avoid holding a whole roll or piece of bread in the palm of your hand and dressing it. Informally English muffins are to be torn in half. Bagels can be cut in half and then torn apart one piece at a time. Then dressed or not each small piece is placed in the mouth with the right hand. There will come a time when as a matter of course, where practical, you do not show teeth marks in what you eat.

A whole loaf of bread can be served at table accompanied by a bread knife and cutting board. The host or senior man can cut slices to start the table. He is to grasp the bread with a clean napkin, cut the loaf in half, turn one half ninety degrees, and at the large side begin cutting it into 3-4 thin slices.

The board and bread may then be passed counter clockwise around the table. Each guest could be allowed to cut each additional slice. Bread is to be present throughout the meal as a viewed symbol of hospitality. The rest of the bread can be admired now and eaten later. It can be shared with staff, or used for croutons or bread pudding by the family. Dream the dream.

Pre-sliced bread is for toast at breakfast and for sandwiches. Commercially, bread served with a meal has been seen to be sliced. This is a deviation allowed for the social good. (It cannot be used as a reason to take back a license.) Trends do not make etiquette.

Butter in dining is to be served in a butter crock set on a table without an underlying plate. It is the second of three items allowed to be placed directly on a table that is not a glass or a plate.

A butter knife (with a point) is to be used to serve butter to a plate. Then the knife is to be placed across the top of the crock.

Casually, butter can be transferred to a B&B plate using a butter spreader (with a rounded top.)

In informal service, each person can take butter from the serving dish with his or her butter spreader. A butter spreader is to be used only for the dressing of breads. It can be rested across the top of a bread and butter plate, blade parallel with the edge of the table or handle at four 'o clock. It may be placed with the handle pointed to one o'clock. (Few do this.) Casually, butter can be spread onto bread with a clean place knife. Commercially, butter can be pre-set at each setting; bread may be served already buttered.

At a formal meal, butter is to be omitted, usually so is the bread and butter plate, and the butter spreader.

Salt Rules

Salt and pepper may be provided by using a salt cellar and a pepper pot. Open salts can be taken with a salt spoon, a clean knife, or with the fingers. Salt could be provided using individual holders or common holders. Salt and pepper can be added to any food item requiring it.

1.   **Taste each food item before adding salt or pepper except for a baked potato, salad,** celery, radishes, a boiled egg, or corn on the cob. Salt that is to be needed for dipping can be placed on the side of the place plate. Salt is to be used sparingly, especially when the cook/host or hostess is sitting at the table.

2.   **When there is a request to, "Pass the salt," both the salt and pepper holders are to be provided. All passing is to be to the right.** Each is to be s**et as a pair in front of each person in turn until reaching the requester.** Reaching at table may now be preferred to asking someone to pass things one can take up.

3.   **Avoid intercepting and using salt being passed to someone else.**

4.   **(Cayenne pepper may be the new salt.)** It can add kick to food and may be helpful in lowering high blood pressure. Pepper could be added to foods as you wish. It might have hidden benefit of being helpful in digestion.

Spoon Rule of Three

Here is how the spoon rules work. The first spoon (1) is to be a (round) soup spoon for cream soup, or a place (table) spoon. When a tablespoon is placed in position #1 it may be for a hearty soup, or a consommé, melon, or at breakfast for cereal.

The second spoon (2) is to be used only for dessert; it can be placed above the plate space, with the handle facing to the right. Yes, informally a teaspoon has been seen used for dessert. It does not make it etiquette.

In formal service, this is a place spoon. A fork to be used with a dessert spoon may be placed below it handle facing to the left.

In a maid-less place setting, the third spoon (3) is (a teaspoon) usually used for something served in a tea cup. It may be placed to the right of the cream soup spoon, or to the right of the last knife when no other spoon is used. It can be omitted from the place setting, until later.

When wishing to employ the rule, to eat, "Go from the outside in," the teaspoon (spoon 3) could be omitted from the place setting, and be brought in when the item requiring it is served.

Spoon rules follow the Flatware Rule of Three: no more than three spoons (or any items of flatware of the same kind) are to be set in any place setting at any one time.

Spoon Rules

When using a spoon alone

1. It is to be placed in the right hand, bowl facing up, with the handle resting on the base knuckle of the index finger, and on the tip knuckle of the middle finger and is to be held in place by the thumb being rested on the face of the handle.

    Avoid the handle being held in the palm of the hand or being held by more than three fingers. You can allow children to teach themselves to do this as long as you remember to unteach it later.

2. A spoon can be used to cut a food item apart (usually fruit,) when held in the right hand, and turned sideways with the face or concave of the bowl facing towards you. The index finger is pressed along the side of the spoon with enough pressure applied to cut the item apart. It can be flexed right or left to complete the item separation.

Spoon Rules for Soup

Soup is to be eaten by using a soup plate, or a cup or soup bowl and an underlying plate, set in a place setting, and a soupspoon.

1. Spoons rules for soup are as follows, start at the table edge of the bowl then, and load the spoon bowl facing away from you. **"As the ship goes out to sea I push spoon my soup away from me."** The spoon is to be placed under the item with the bowl facing toward the center of the table. It is filled and leveled.

2. A spoon may be tipped away from you against the front of the vessel to allow any excess amounts of the item to be returned. It can be rested in place just above the vessel the item was taken from. It can be filled and in mock baby feeding form drawn across the right edge of the plate or bowl.

3. Only the first third of the spoon is to enter the mouth from the tip or from the side of it. Three teaspoons equal a tablespoon; thus in formal service a tablespoon is to be used for dessert. Liquid is to be let into the mouth from the side of a spoon in small silent pours. You can close your mouth over the spoon and take a small portion of a solid item.

4. **Avoid blowing on a spoonful of soup,** (the same as for coffee.) A spoon can be used to stir soup to cool and to test the temperature of it. Then it is again leveled before the food item is taken to the mouth from the side of the spoon. Avoid blowing on a spoon. (You would not do it to a fork.)

5. The spoon rest position is center the vessel handle pointed to four o'clock.

6. **The spoon in the finished position**, when used in a soup plate, is to be placed **bowl center the plate, handle pointed to four o'clock.** The finished position for a spoon, when used with a cup or bowl is to the right side **on the underlying plate or saucer.**

An Advanced Formal Place Setting

In an advanced "formal" place setting, typically, left to right flatware can consist of a fish or appetizer fork, a place (or meat) course fork, a salad fork, and (above a plate) a dessert spoon handle pointed to the right. And maybe under it a dessert fork handle pointed to the left. Then to the right side of the plate there can be a salad knife, a place (or meat) knife, a fish or appetizer knife, a soupspoon, and an oyster cocktail fork. It can be placed to the left of other forks.

Each course is to get its own glass and flatware placed in order of use outside in – in kind, **(all knives and then a spoon.)** And know the rule of four: of the five glasses no more than four are to be set in a place setting at any one time. The glass for the soup course is usually omitted.

The rule, "Go from the outside in-in kind" is understood to mean the coffee spoon is omitted from the place setting. **It can be brought in when coffee is served.** Set all forks, knives, and then one spoon. And then when the table is set to a menu, "Go from the outside in" in kind. In a formal place setting, butter is to be omitted from the menu. The rule, "Eat from the outside in," is understood to mean when a spoon for dessert is not required, is set above the plate space handle pointed to the right, or will be brought in when the course is served.

Set all forks, knives, and then all spoons. And then when the table is set to a menu, "Go from the outside in" in kind. In a formal place setting, butter is to be omitted from the menu.

At a Formal Place Setting table, avoid making personal items: books or technology apart of a cover.

In a private home, allow the senior woman to pick up flatware first. This is a universal indicator; others are to do so.

A **service plate** or **charger** can be placed at the center of each place setting before people come to the table. This plate is normally larger than a main course or place plate, and it has a one-inch colored rim. It is sometimes called a **"Show plate."**

In a commercial environment, a service plate can be used for every meal except breakfast. It has been introduced and can be used as a buffet plate. In a private home, it is used in formal United States of America service. The crest, if any, is to face the edge of the table.

A show plate can be used to set the underlying plate for the first and second course. It can stay in service until a main course plate is served. A napkin is placed center the service plate when the first course is to be served later. The service plate may be omitted.

An Advanced Formal Place Setting
W/ a charger or show plate

Name Each Glass

Know the name of each glass -- left to right Water, Red wine, White wine, and Champagne (the fluted glass above the others.) A Sherry glass has been omitted.

Know the rule of four: of the five no more than (four) glasses are to be set in a place setting at any one time. Each is to be placed according to the size of the plate and order of the course to be used with it.

Flatware Etiquette Rule of Three & Rule of Ten

The line to the food begins with the menu order of courses. Flatware is to be set on a table based on a menu. It can be a road map to a meal: what courses will be served and when.

Have no fear. In an advanced formal place setting, there is a flatware rule of three: no more than three items of flatware of any one kind are to be placed in any place setting at any one time. An oyster cocktail fork can be placed with up to three other forks in a place setting. It is the lone exception to the rule of three. It can be placed to the left of other forks or tines in the bowl of the soup spoon handle to five o'clock.

And then there is the rule of ten: no more than ten pieces of flatware of any kind are to be placed at one place setting at any given time.

Each course is to get its own flatware placed in order of use outside in – in kind: all knives and then all spoons.

Study place settings even when alone. There are other flatware combinations of ten. Each is an informal place setting. In a formal place setting, not only is the bread and butter plate and butter spreader to be omitted from a place setting, but **after some point, additional flatware items can be brought in with the course requiring it.**

Being Excruciatingly Fork Literate

It is my wish to assist you in being excruciatingly fork literate and considerate. About forks, in current use there are six. You know them as this:

1. Oyster cocktail
2. Appetizer
3. Fish w/ a notched left tine
4. Meat/ Main Course/Place/Dinner
5. Salad
6. Dessert

Someone will tell you about an olive, pickle, butter, and an ice cream fork, so there are at least ten. But if you do not already have them, chances are if you see them; they cannot be obtained, and if they could very few would know how or when to use them.

Polished Table Manners

Notes to Self - Acquire Polished Table Manners

In home training, the quantity of food you eat will endear you to someone. In public life, it is the style in which you eat that will do the same thing.

"Eat a little something after leaving home." Order something easy: that you know how to eat. Before a public meal is the time you can use that meal deal fast food coupon.

At home, practice eating chicken with a knife and fork. Under a roof, it is the etiquette. You can be good at it.

Even when alone, avoid wearing headphones, a hat, or a backpack at table.

At a public event you can have a name badge where it up high to make yourself known. When you are an escort it may read, "Ask me about… an organization, product, company, or specialty."

Establish and maintain your place setting or cover. *Leave the centerpiece alone.*

Avoid eating with or books or technology in one hand and food or drink in the other. These items can be set at table after you finish your meal.

Look for food to be served (counter clockwise) from the left (leaving side) of the place setting. **Pass to the right where applicable. Say, "May I" "Please" "Thank you" and "Welcome," as appropriate.**

In public, when served too much food you can ask for or get another plate. Use the first plate as a serving dish. Serve a portion of each item to the new plate.

Items left in a serving dish can be considered leftovers. Items left on a plate from which someone has eaten are table scraps. Whoever eats the latter is to remember the bag was meant for the dog. When you can, avoid asking for leftovers at any place other than with family.

Wait for most everyone to be served before eating. Eat in an established style; learn how. Learn the art of cutting meat without sawing it; avoid sawing cooked dead meat.

Avoid the dunk or the duck and chuck: ducking your head down to meet your food, and chucking it into your mouth. Sit up straight. Put your back into it. Eat with your neck up. Bring food to you. Monitor ingestion: time the opening of your mouth to just coincide with the arrival of an implement or food to your month. Close your mouth around the edge of any implement placed in it. Avoid the bump: a visible lump of food in your cheek. Chew each portion twenty-four times. Taste buds live and digestion begins in the mouth. Around chew seven-teen, you will experience a taste explosion. Cool, now blot your mouth with a napkin and taste the water.

Pace yourself. *Each course is to be eaten at a pace even with the person to your right side.* ***"Can I take that for you?" could be code for, "You ate that (way) too fast."*** *The time it takes to eat a meal is to be at least half the total time it took to make it, even a thirty minute meal, is to take more time to eat than the time it takes to plate.*

In public, leave a little of each course on your plate, and a little of each drink in each glass. When finished each course plate (and centerpiece) is to be left in a picture ready condition. Avoid seconds in any home not your own. Bus your table between courses. (Take each finished plate away from the table, each time you return with a fresh one.)

Leave telephone on vibrate. If you have to leave the table to telephone, text, or to handle something on your own, leave between courses where possible. Place your napkin on your chair. Say, "Excuse me." Push in your chair – when you can.

You can have a travel toothbrush in your pocket when you plan to brush your teeth, after the salad (4th) course or after the meal. When in public, step away from the sink when brushing your teeth to allow access to those who are just washing hands. You can do other checks and repairs prior to returning to the table.

OK now you can bus that last plate and glass if you must (when a staff member has not been hired to do so.)

Stand and push in your chair – when you can. The plate is to be carried in your left hand and the glass in your right hand. The glass can be carried rested on the palm of the left hand. The table can be crumbed with a napkin in the right hand; both are to be placed under the plate. Avoid making garbage plates. Acquire polished table manners; to do these things, you may need to take an etiquette tour or lesson on Professional and Graduate University Etiquette Business Dining. Good for you.

Second Helpings

The hostess (or the host) is to be allowed to decide if seconds at table are to be offered.*

1.   In a private home, seconds are offered only of the main dish.

2.   After accepting an offer of seconds, when carving is done at the table, pass your plate with the used flatware in the finished position placed atop it, to the host or the original server.

3.   Seconds can be served Family style: the serving dish and implements may be passed to the person who accepted an offer of a dish.

4.   A hostess is to eat slowly enough to keep company with any person eating seconds. She can elect to take a second of the main course item to do this.

5. In a commercial dining room, seconds of rolls, (sliced bread,) or butter can be accomplished by exchanging an empty container with a filled one.

6. Water is offered at least once after the service of the main course. Get a pitcher. You may use that 32 oz container as one.

7. In public life, avoid asking for and/or accepting seconds where possible. At formal meals (and public dinners) seconds are not properly offered (nor asked for.)

Avoid eating seconds in any home not your own. (Eating is not to be the reason for the meeting.) Refuse seconds albeit politely, even when the hostess insists. You may regret this at first and then be pleasantly surprised by a great dessert.

*Note: "Seconds" can be leftovers for meals for school, work, or dinner for tomorrow. They may be a meal for staff tonight. – Besides, you already followed rule #1 and ate, "a little something before getting there."

Using Cutlery Eating USA Style

When eating in the "American Style"

1.   The spoon when used is to be held in the right hand bowl up.

It can be filled with the bowl facing away from the table. In the rest position it is placed diagonally center the bowl or soup plate, bowl facing up, handle pointed to four o'clock, (in the ten-twenty position.) In the finished position it is to be placed to the right side of a soup plate handle to four o'clock or when used with a bowl the handle is to be placed on an underlying plate at six o'clock.

2.   The fork when used is to be held in the right hand tines up, handle pointed to four o'clock. It is to rest on the tip knuckle of the middle finger and on the base knuckle of the index finger, held in place by the thumb rested on the face of the handle. In the finished position it is to be placed to the right side of a plate at handle at four o'clock or six o'clock.

The fork alone can be used to cut a food item apart. To cut an item a fork can be turned sideways with the face facing adjacent to the edge of the table. The index finger is placed along the side of the fork and pressed down with enough pressure to cut the item being parted.

It can be flexed right or left to complete the item separation. The fork is then righted and the item is impaled or picked up. The tines are filled, lifted, and held in place for an extended second or drawn to the side of the plate before the food item is taken to the mouth. The item is to be taken from the front of the fork.

Avoid holding a fork standing up in any plate.

At table, a fork is to be used when putting butter on vegetables and jellies on meat. It can be used to move food items to the right third of the plate to store a portion to be cut later. It may be used to move items to the left of the plate to be discarded. Once used, the fork is to be placed in the rest position for it. Avoid resting it like an oar pair in a rowboat.

In the American Style of eating, bread is sometimes seen used to push food inconspicuously onto a fork. Avoid this practice.

The bottom of the fork tines can be used to move a food item to the work area of the plate and pressed down on the food item ever so gently; the item affixed to the bottom of the fork may be placed in the mouth.

A fork can be used in conjunction with a knife to cut a food item apart. To **cut food with a knife and fork, the fork is to be held in the left hand handle to palm, tines down,** and the index finger extended along the back of it.

The fork in is to be used to impale and to hold in place the item to be cut. It can be used to secure and to move the item to the front third of the plate facing the edge of the table. This area is to be used to slice the item being cut.

3.   **The knife is to be grasped in the right hand handle to palm,** blade down, and the index finger extended along the back of it. The right thumb is to be stretched straight and is to rest on the inner side of the knife handle.

The **blade is to be placed in front of the tines of the fork,** without touching them. The knife is to be used for cutting the item apart one or two pieces at a time.

Let the cutting begin: the blade is to be pressed down on the item from the tip of the blade, with enough pressure to cut the item, and then drawn toward the edge of the table with one or two strokes all in one direction. It can be flexed towards the fork and any bone to complete the item separation. This process may be repeated as required. (Avoid sawing cooked food.) Cut one to two pieces at a time in only one direction.

If you cut more than one or two pieces at a time, someone may get you that bib and a Sippy cup, and have at hand a nappy change: a Huggie or depends, or think to and not tell you; "That's how we feed the baby."

4. **Eating US American Style – after cutting the item apart, the knife is placed on the cut piece as the fork is withdrawn from it. Then it is placed in diagonally across top right hand part of the plate blade facing the table handle at two o'clock.**

5. Avoid facing the blade away from the plate – as if you are going to strike someone. Avoid confusing a knife for an oar in a rowboat - or resting one like one.

6. Next, the fork is switched from the left hand to right hand, the left hand is placed on the lap, and tines' facing up the fork is to be used to,

   Load: impale or pick up the food item onto the fork tines.

   Lock: bring the fork to the work area: bottom third of the plate. Hold it in place for an extended second or draw it to the side of the plate.

   Lift: **turn the wrist in and upward and take the item to the mouth.**

7.   After the food item is eaten the fork is switched back to the left hand, unless placed in the rest position. The rest position for the fork is the tines up center the plate, handle pointed to four o'clock. The rest position allows you to take in conversation, to chew, to tear off and eat a piece of bread, and/or to blot your mouth with a napkin prior to taking a drink of water or wine.

8.   You can take a hand rest often. In this style, Keep one hand (usually your left) off the table: in your lap with a napkin. A hand in the lap without a napkin is suspect. The right wrist may be rested on the edge of the table.

When required, the knife can be picked up in the right hand and the cutting process may be repeated as long as the item remains. The knife can be used to add butter to bread, when a butter spreader has been omitted.

9.   The finished position for the fork is placed center the plate tines up handle pointed to four o'clock or six o'clock.

The finished position for the knife is to the right of the fork with the blade edge facing towards it. The fork can be placed tines up to the right side of the plate, handle pointed toward the edge of the table at six o'clock. The knife is placed to the right side of it, rested on the edge of the plate. Avoid placing used flatware back on the table, where possible.

10. A plate fork and knife are to be used collectively--silently. As much as possible, avoid letting others hear the meal you are eating. If not required, flatware is to be left in the place in which it was set.

11. For dessert a spoon takes the place of a knife and is used to cut an item. It is also used to eat the item. Class begins and ends with a spoon.

Note. In a private home, flatware that appears unclean can be used in silence. You could play, "Clumsy me," and say, "I dropped my (whatever.)"

The replacement item may be equally unclean. In a commercial dining room, you might ask the host or hostess for a replacement without additional comment.

And no, you cannot ask for and then clean your flatware with a lemon. What are you trying to say to others at your table; (avoid doing this at your own risk, or it's OK for them to get sick? Stop it.) (You cannot sanitize flatware with a napkin anyway.)

Eating Continental Style

When Eating Continental style, keep both of your hands on the table: wrists on or above the table edge, and your napkin on your lap.

1. The place fork and knife are to be grasped handles in the palm of the left and right hands, **index fingers along the backs of both handles.**

    When a food item is to be cut, the fork is picked up in the left hand. The tines are to be placed face down and are used to **impale the item** to be cut. The knife blade is to be set in front of the tip of the fork without touching it. Let the cutting begin; to affect a cut the blade is pressed down on the item from the tip of the blade, with pressure enough to cut the item, and flexed towards the fork and any bone, and then drawn toward the edge of the table with one or two strokes all in one direction. It can be flexed away from the fork again to complete the item separation. This process may be repeated as required. Cutting is to be done only in one direction.

■   **Eating Continental Style – after the food item is cut, the knife is to remain in the right hand.**   Next, with the fork tines face down,

- **a. Load: impale or place the food item onto the back of the fork tines with the knife.**

- **b. Lock:** bring the fork to the work area: bottom third of the plate. Hold it in place for an extended second or draw it to the side of the plate.

- **c. Lift: turn the wrist in and upward and take the item to the mouth.**

2.   **After, the food item is eaten the knife remains in the right hand,** unless it is placed in the rest position for it: **knife handle pointed to four o'clock.** The fork remains in the left hand throughout the meal, unless it is placed in the rest position for it: fork handle at eight o'clock, tines over the knife blade.

3.   You can take a hand rest often. The heel of your palms can rest in your lap (USA) or on the edge of the table.

4.   For a non-main dish item, **the knife is correctly used as to push or to pull food onto the back of the fork and to press it down to one side. Then with the wrist turned up, the fork can be used to balance the food item to be taken to the mouth.**

5.   The finished position for the fork is tines down, center the plate handle pointed to four o'clock. The finished position for the knife is to the right of the fork with the blade edge facing towards it. The fork can be placed tines down to the right side of the plate, handle pointed toward the edge of the table. The knife is to be placed to the right side of it, rested on the edge of the plate.

6.   The fork or spoon when used alone is to be held in the right hand tines or bowl up.

      In the rest and the finished position, each is placed diagonally center the plate tines or bowl up handle pointed to four o'clock (in the ten-twenty position.) In the finished position each can be placed to the right side of the plate handles pointed to six o'clock.

7.   **Pace yourself. Caution – this style is quieter and more efficient. It can allow you to finish very fast. Take your time. "Can I take that for you?" can be code for, "You ate that way too fast.**

8.   You can eat in a style indicated by your host. You can also be very polished at it.

Flatware **Rest Positions**

In the United States American Style of Eating the **rest position for the knife is blade** placed **diagonally across the top right-hand part of the plate, facing toward the table, handle pointed to two o'clock.**

The rest position for the fork is the tines up center the plate, handle pointed to four o'clock.

In the Continental Style of Eating th**e rest position for the knife handle pointed to four o'clock, fork handle at eight o'clock, tines over the knife blade.**

The rest position allows you to take in conversation, to chew, eat a piece of bread, and to blot your mouth with a napkin prior to taking a drink of water or wine. And to wait for those who do not eat as fast or as efficiently as you do.

The Line to the Food

The Line to the Food A Main Course

Avoid calling a main course an entrée. Outside of a commercial dining room, and in a polite world, an entrée comes before one. A main course is to be

1. A (Roti) or roasted meat or poultry item.
2. A fish item can be served as a main course item.
3. Tofu may be served as a main course.
4. A baked vegetable item could be served as one.

Each main course is to be eaten using a knife and a fork.

1. It is to be sliced, cut, and eaten from the "Work" area of the plate: the portion closest to the table. The fork is to be used to hold the item in place. The item is to be sliced with grain, and cut across the grain, into manageable portions one or two pieces at a time.

2. When the main course item is meat or poultry it can be pressed with a knife to cut the item, and flicked towards the fork and any bone present all at one time, and then cut again as each piece is desired during the course.

   Any bone, skin, gristle, and any unwanted portion may be pressed, cut and flicked away, and picked up by using a fork, or a fork and a knife, and placed to the left side of the plate. At a table, avoid using your fingers to pick up the bone(s) of a meat or poultry item to eat or to gnaw at any remaining meat.

A Burrito

A Burrito is a meal wrapped in a Tortilla. Burritos are foods in wrapping for a working man on the run. Each use to contain only one item and were a whole lot smaller.

A Tortilla is essentially a food wrapper. A wrapper when seated is to be used as a plate. Tortillas are essentially bread that is made of fat cut into stripped wheat flour that is that is served half done. When hot items are placed inside it, it starts to return to goo. Wheat is to be fully cooked. Yes, they know that is why you may order a fried Burrito bowl.

You can use your Tortilla as bread. You may order corn tortilla instead. You could open up your Grande Burrito. Use and knife and fork and enjoy the inside. Get out the good stuff, and then decide if I want to eat that gooey wheat, that is left on your plate. You can leave it there. Stay thin enough to enjoy your date.

Tortillas were traditionally made of corn. Look it up. Love cooked tortillas and corn chips with and without dips.

You can sit and eat a burrito Grande: essentially a whole meal in your hand. But you cannot a**void showing teeth marks in bread you are eating. Once you know the rule, what you do is up to you. Do this under a roof and someone will remember to give you your sugar cube.**

Pizza Manners

Pizza can be served as a main course on a serving dish. Pizza is to be served with sides: soup,   wings, crudités, hummus, salad, or fruit, and a cookie or ice cream.

In public, avoid eating pizza directly from a box. Pizza is not to be sopped with paper napkins to drain off the oils, (something I have seen,) and this is not a request normally asked for from a kitchen.

Under a roof, pizza is to be eaten from a plate placed center each place setting, from an established cover: with a plate, fork, and a knife; optionally, a glass is to be placed above the knife space to the right of the plate space, and with a napkin placed on the lap.

Pizza can be eaten with a knife and fork. This is normally reserved for a deep dish pie, or one with a running sauce. It may be reserved for when pizza is topped with Arugula and fresh tomatoes; even then it is a personal choice. Informally, pizza may be placed on a plate and eaten with the fingers. Each side may be bent upwards and the wedge taken to the mouth and pizza eaten one bite at a time. The braces I am sure are already paid for, and you may want to show off your marks.

Pizza may be pre-cut into squares and used as a cocktail food, held on a plate, with it and a napkin and drink in one hand, as practice for a real cocktail party.

Spaghetti Manners

Spaghetti is to be eaten using a fork alone. In a private home, spaghetti has been seen eaten using a fork and a spoon. The fork is held in the right hand. It is used to select a few strands of spaghetti. The spoon is held in the left hand. It is used as a base for the fork to assist in the winding of the spaghetti around it. The spoon is then rested on the upper right side of the plate: in the rest position for a knife. A fork has been seen being twirled against a small piece of bread to assist the winding process. In more formal settings, the use of a spoon and/or bread is to be avoided.

In public, Spaghetti is to be eaten using a fork alone.

1.   A space is to be made to the bottom of the plate. The fork is to be used to select a few strands.

2.   Then in the bare space it is twined silently around and around until all the strands in the group have been wound around it.

3.   The filled fork is to be rested, brought to the front of the plate, folded to the side, and then taken to the mouth. This process is to be repeated for the rest of the dish. The fork alone or the fork and the spoon can be used to mix the sauce and cheese onto the spaghetti. The used spoon is then rested in the rest position for it. Then eat.

How to Eat Chicken Bone In with a Knife and Fork

The rule, when chicken is to be eaten under a roof, it is to be eaten with a knife and a fork. It is no longer a finger food. Even the Colonel provides plates, knives, and forks, and Staff will ask, "Will this be "To go" or for our dining room?" The company knows the rule. After you are asked, what you do with that box or bucket reflects on you. What to do

1.   Establish a cover: a place setting for one. Serve a plate. Practice your "Chicken manners."

2.   The portion to be eaten is placed in the "work" bottom area of the plate. You've seen the pictures. The skin can be removed by the fork being used to hold the item in place, and the knife being used to cut the end of it. Then it may be used to gently roll the skin back towards the back of the fork. The skin could be set aside to the right to be eaten later or to the left to be discarded.

3.   **The chicken piece is to be impaled with the fork held in the left hand and cut: pressed from the tip of the knife in the right, and then a small piece can be flicked gently away from the fork and any bone. More delicately now, the meat is to be sliced with the grain and cut across it into manageable portions one or two pieces at a time. Then the fork is used to lift each portion to the mouth.**

4.   Chicken joined by a joint can be separated by the fork being used to hold the item in place and the knife at the joint being pressed down to feel the join, then drawn backwards, and pressed to cut the item into separate parts. It can be pressed down and gently flicked towards the fork and any bone to complete the joint separation. Then pieces might be sliced, cut, and eaten.

5.   The part of the chicken that cannot be pressed, flicked away, and sliced with a knife and fork is simply left, at least 'til you get to the kitchen.

———————

Small poultry items can be eaten as much as practical with a knife and fork and then finished with the fingers. When served cold, at picnics, at the beach, on boats, and during very informal meals outside, even chicken may be eaten with the fingers.

Welcome to your business dinner. Most likely the main course will be a half of a (rubber) chicken or a whole Cornish game hen. Now, are not you happy you practiced?

Handling Mishaps at the Table

1. A bad item is to be spooned out of a soup dish and onto an underlying plate. Where necessary, it can be dropped to the floor using your hand, and the spoon is to be placed in the finished position for the dish. Avoid telling the event host that a bad item was found in your soup.

2. In a commercial dining room, a fly is to be spooned out of a soup dish and hidden discreetly. It can be put in a pocket. The commercial host and/or the board of health may be told of this incident at a more convenient time. For right now, the spoon is to be placed in the finished position for the dish.

3. A bad item can be pushed out of the mouth and onto a spoon or fork. Bad items can include gristle, or a piece of meat, that you chewed into as small a piece as possible, but cannot swallow. The same eating style and implement used to eat the item is be used to remove it.

    A bad item can be removed by using a spoon bowl up or a fork, tines up in the United States of America style, or with fork tines down in the Continental style. Then it is placed on the left side of the plate.

4. A hostess who notices an untouched dish can say, "Do let me serve you a fresh portion," and have the dish or drink replaced without remarking as to the need for the replacement.

5.   A bad item is to be screened, if possible, with a garnish or a piece of bread. An exception to this rule is small pieces of oyster shell, olive pits, eggshell, bone, and birds. Each can be removed with the fingers. When in desperate straits, the thumb and index fingers are used to transfer an item from the mouth to the left side of the plate. The fingertips are then rubbed across the corner of a napkin. If you

6.   Inadvertently burp or your stomach growls say, "Excuse me." When about to burp, cover your mouth and expend the air as quietly as possible. Then say, "Excuse me." Avoid dwelling on these things.

7.   When you break a glass or plate say, "I am sorry." Offer to replace the item. You can hope that you are assured that there is, "No reason." **A guest is responsible for damages he or she is party to while being entertained**. Take care of any replacement item provided. The hostess can still wish that you were a tad less clumsy.

8.   When you are about to sneeze turn your head and cover your nose with a handkerchief. While sneezing make as little noise as possible. Then say, "Excuse me." Avoid dwelling on it. When someone else does it say, "Bless you." This response is to be "Thank you." You can squelch or suppress a sneeze by taking any finger and pressing the skin directly under the center of your nose.

9. When about to cough cover your mouth with the top of a closed fist or with a bend in the elbow. At the first sign that something more is about to happen, assume that approval to leave the table is granted. Proffer, "Excuse me" upon your return.

10. When food rolls or falls off your plate and onto the table, pick it up. Use any utensil available. Return it to the left "Discard" side of your plate. When food rolls onto the floor, you can nonchalantly reach down, pick it up, and keep it in your napkin. In a commercial dining room, you can cover it with your "Dropped" napkin and then request a new one. The host is to let the server know that a new one is now required.

11. A water glass that has been knocked over is to be set right. The spilled water is to be allowed to be absorbed into the tablecloth. Omit the word, "Oops." Someone may get a cloth and place over (or to wipe) it. To that person say, "Thank you." When you spill something on another person say, "I am sorry." Offer this person your napkin. Let the person handle his or her own wiping or blotting. You can say, "Let me pay for the dry cleaning."

12. A wet napkin may be used to wipe a spot on a tablecloth, garment, or skin. Remember, water and the corner of a napkin can be used to correct a multitude of at table sins.

Salad Rules

Salad can be the fourth course. **Fancy as it gets – salads' purpose ultimately is to push away the main course before it. It is to be offered and served after it or with it. It can be better to wait until after you eat, or it snows, before you plow the road.** "Avoid spending your whole life eating your entrée (main course) with the third fork."

Salad is to be green leaves served with cheese and crackers. It can be pre-plated on a salad plate, or served in a salad bowl without an underlying plate. It is the third of three items allowed to be placed directly on a table that is not a glass or a plate. Informally, salad could be served from a large bowl passed counter clockwise around the table with attending implements used to place salad onto a plate or into a bowl. Salad is to be dressed by using a set of cruets: one for oil and the other for vinegar. Pepper can be added to taste. This process is to be completed as quickly as possible. A salad dressing can be served in a small bowl with an underlying plate and a ladle, and ladled onto the salad. In some commercial dining rooms, salad dressing is placed onto the salad before it is set on the table. Croutons can be served offered or pre-placed on salad.

Note: Salad served with large leaves, with cheese, or in a rocklike quarter head is to be eaten by using a knife and a fork. Salad may be cut using the side of the fork.

Each leaf can be picked up, or rolled back and impaled, on the tines of the fork and taken to the mouth. If the salad can be cut with the edge of the salad fork alone, the clean salad knife can remain on the table.

Informally, salad might be served as a first course placed center the place setting. Salad can be served in a bowl or on a plate. The plate for the course can be set atop a show plate. A bowl when used for salad can be set directly onto a table, tablecloth, or on a placemat. A salad bowl is the only bowl that can be correctly placed on a table directly without an underlying doily or plate.

When salad is to be served as a first course, cheese is to be omitted. Informally salad can be served at the same time as the main course. It may be placed on a dinner plate wherever space allows. It could be a non-green salad served without crackers or cheese. Each small tomato can be pierced with the end tine of a fork.

Salad served in a very large individual bowl can be plated to a smaller bowl or to a plate. Avoid looking as if you are eating out of a salad container. When salad is served in a Soup plate, or your meal is served in a bowl without an underlying plate, be cautious what you get for dessert, you may be given a treat.

Still ordering salad before meat, take another dining class before you eat. Salad before meat with creamy dressing "to go with that," may ruin your palate and make you fat. Practice," Salad after meat;" this is the order, even in America at the White House as listed on each State dinner menu that I have seen (except one.)

Salad is for cleaning the system, not for cleansing the palate. It can be assisted by oil and vinegar. Salad served after the main course is to include cheese and crackers. You may add some pepper to it. It is said, each can aid with digestion. This course can be skipped at a business dinner or on a date, in favor of a dessert.

The Line to the Bathroom

The line to the bathroom is to be used to lead people to the best looking bathroom in the house by the most direct route. A bathroom can be used before one comes to the table. It may be used after ordering a drink at any place serving as a bar.

- The trip could begin with the statement, "I'll be right back," or with the question, "Where can I wash my hands," after reading any reusable menu. Expect a visit to station six: the bathroom.

- At a banquet, during the intermission, this is where you can take that five to ten minute break. It could be used to allow each person to make repairs to body, mind, and/or make up, to check nails, and to mark cards.

In a private home, upon entering the bathroom

1. Lock the door. If you are modest, (or well bred,) you can turn on the water. Men are to sit and point. Make as little noise as possible.

2.   While inside, strive to eliminate any odor not considered desirable. You can light a single sulfur match (if anyone still has them.) Blow it out. Hold it until the smoke dissipates and then deposit it in an ashtray or in the toilet and flush.

You may search for and use an air freshener to spray the water in a short burst. (Yes, it works.) I hide it at the back of the toilet. Spray the water and then under the seat. You could spray it with a breath spray, or add a drop or two of cologne or a few drops of liquid soap. Then flush again. The room will smell better. You might then spray the air.

Hands are to be washed each time after finishing in the bathroom. Turn on the faucet at least once while in the bathroom. Wet the soap, if only to make someone believe that before leaving you really did wash your hands and that you do deserve to eat off of china plates. It is easier just to do it.

1.   Wash your hands with cold water and soap. (It releases the grease and the soap.)

2.   Turn off the water. You can wipe out the sink using toweling or toilet tissue: watch the shine! Place the trash in a receptacle, and leave the bathroom ready to receive the next person. Bless you.

On the way out of the bathroom, there are things you can do

1.   Look for a body or hand lotion. Use some: on your face, lips and hands.

2.   Check the mirror. Look at your nose. Then look at your mouth and teeth. Check for particles of foodstuff.

3.   Look for that wrapped toothpick. Use it. You can carry a travel toothbrush, and plan for a way to brush your teeth after you eat, with or without paste.

4.   Look for a dish of wrapped signature candy. Have one.

5.   Look for a single rose or flower taken from the centerpiece. Smell it.

6.   Take time to look at each candle lit and floating in a tub. This can be both safe and look awesome.

7.   O.K., it is time to leave, back to your dinner table.

Note: The bathroom is the only room in which you get to be alone. It is where you get to inspect the environment and make decisions about the host from a sitting position. There are nineteen things you can place in a bathroom for someone else. Remember this when you get home.

Note: This page is a breach of etiquette: "What is done behind the door of a bathroom is private." Yes, it is, until another person is listening or enters the room. In a commercial environment, when an attendant is present, services are to be used and tipped.

Eating Dessert

Dessert can be the (fifth or) last course. It is to be served at all meals when company is in attendance. It is to be ordered only if the host does. Dessert can be served in a saucer champagne glass or in a bowl set atop an underlying (B&B) plate. It may be served on a salad plate. A dessert plate, empty or filled, can be passed to each person at a table and set center the place setting. Sauce for a dessert is to be served in a sauce boat and stand and ladled onto it. Sauce can be pre-ladled onto a dessert. Prior to serving dessert, the table is to be "corrected." In banquet service, this is what happens while you take that "Five to ten minute break."

Flatware for the dessert can be preset set at table. A spoon can be preset above the plate: handle pointed to the right. A fork may be placed under a spoon handle to the left. What to do? **Bring the flatware items to the sides of the plate: the fork to the left and/ or the spoon to the right.** A spoon could be placed to the left of the first (soup) spoon, and or to the right of the last knife when placed alone. A fork could be placed to the right of the last fork.

Dessert flatware can be brought in when the course is served set in place center each place setting. It can consist of a plate passed with a doily and a finger bowl placed atop it, and flatware placed on each side of it. Flatware is to be provided with a finger bowl only for dessert. What to do? Each person at table is to

1. Place the doily and the finger bowl just above the space for the fork.

2. The fork is to be set to the left of the plate.

3. The spoon is set to the right.

The dessert course can be eaten using a fork and spoon, a fork or spoon alone, or with the fingers alone.

1. A fork and spoon can be used together for a dessert course. The spoon takes the place of and is to be used as a knife. The fork is used tines down to hold the item in place while it is being cut. The fork can be used as a pusher to push-pull an item onto a spoon. The spoon is to be used to eat the item. In the Continental style the left hand is kept above the table. When a fork or spoon is used alone each is to be held in the right hand tines or bowl up. A fork alone is to be used to cut and eat cake that is frosted.

2. Fingers can be used to eat unfrosted cake; the thumb, index, and the middle fingers may be used to break off a piece of cake and to take it to your mouth.

Eating Crème Brulee

Crème brulee is to be eaten by using a ramekin, an underlying plate set in a place setting, and a spoon.

1.   The cup can be steadied with the left hand. The side of the spoon is used to tap or to crack the sugar crust shell.

2.   The top shell is pushed into the crème.

3.   The dish to be eaten by being spooned from the shell and placed into the mouth.

4.   The finished position for the spoon is to the right side of the cup atop the underlying plate.

When garnished with berries (and kiwi) each is to be eaten with a spoon.

Dessert Flatware Rest and Positions

4. **In the United States of America eating style, when eating dessert, the rest position for the fork is tines up to the left side of the plate; handle pointed to the edge of the table. The rest position for the spoon is to the right side of the plate; handle pointed in the same direction.**

5. The finished position for the fork is tines up to the right side of the plate handle pointed to four o'clock. It can be placed handle pointed toward the edge of the table. The finished position for the spoon is the right side of the fork parallel to it.

6. **In the Continental eating style when eating dessert, the rest position for the spoon is center of the plate bowl up handle pointed to four o'clock. The rest position for the fork is tines down over the bowl of the spoon; handle to the left pointed to eight o'clock.**

7. When the spoon and fork are used together, the finished position for the fork is tines down handle pointed to four o'clock. It can be placed handle toward the edge of the table. The spoon is placed bowl up to the right side of the fork and parallel to it.

Drinks with Dessert

Champagne can be served as a dessert wine. Sparkling water, or cider, may be served in lieu of it

Coffee may be served with dessert or after it. It can be omitted.

At Table Meal Finishes

All finished? The plate for a one-course meal or for the last course is to be left center the place setting until after you get up from or leave the table. Flatware is to be placed in the finished position for the style in which you are eating.

Eating continentally fork tines down, eating American style tines up. Both styles, handle to four o'clock, knife to the right of the fork blade facing it. Flatware that is not used is to be left on the table. In a commercial dining room, it means that the item the flatware piece was intended to be used with was omitted. In a private home, it means that the guest did an "Oops", or the knife was not needed to cut the salad. Someone will check. Life will go on. Real trash can be placed under the left section of the plate. Each beverage glass left is to be in the place setting position for it.
You can ask people at table to sign a menu card, set by each woman, and keep it as a memento. For this have a pen.

Keep your napkin on your lap, until the hostess or the senior woman at the table places her's on the table to the left. Following this lead, place your **napkin in a mock fold to the left of your place setting**.

Remain in your chair until the hostess or the senior woman at the table places her napkin on the table to her left and rises to leave. Then get up with alacrity and grace. Assist any woman to your right in getting up. Pull out her chair. Allow her to exit the space. Then push her **chair in to a point six inches from the table edge.** Now do the same to your chair. Leave the table in honor order.

For practice, go back to chair and take a picture of your cover. It is to be ready to receive seconds or do it over. Avoid making a trash plate or a plate trash. That finished view is what someone can think of you.

The Line to Take Aways

■ In company, a**void asking for or making a doggie bag.** (For this you may wait until after you graduate.)

In business and at a banquet, the line to the leftovers is usually omitted. Food is to be eaten or not in place. In business, avoid asking for or accepting invitations to take food home.

The take-way can be **a party favor, a memento to take home: a menu card (have it signed,) a photograph, a small present, or newly acquired information: sales pitch – training – contacts, and notes. It may be just lots of notes.**

The Line to Good bye
The First Half of Saying Thank You Physical Acknowledgement

Job Interview tip:

The first half of saying "Thank You" acknowledgement is done in two parts: physical attendance and saying thank you.

Part a. Show up. Meet expectations in dress and deportment.

Part b. Say, "Thank you" for every event you attend where you did not have to work or pay to attend, say thank you to the host or hostess in person.

You can say, "Thank you for inviting me," "Thank you for a wonderful evening," or "Thank You for the interview." Make it so that your host or hostess is able to say, "I am so glad that you came."

Hearing, "I am so "very" glad that you came," is not the same thing.

When not a business meal, In a commercial environment, when you receive food raw, well done, brunt, stale, old, or salted like a pretzel, you can save a piece (and take a picture) in case you want to tell someone later.

You may send a portion back to be packed "To go" so you can do something with it later: have it to make a stew for the host, or a gift for the health department.

There is more than one way to say, "Thank you so very much, for having me."

Saying Thank You II A Note by Hand

The second half of saying "Thank You" is done is two parts, written acknowledgement and reciprocity

Part a. is written acknowledgement: when you get home, write a Thank you note by hand. You can send the host or hostess a nice but short thank you note by hand for every event you attend, where work, or payment, was not required. You can send the interviewer a note saying thank you for the interview. This is one of the reasons for getting the business card.

A pre-printed thank you card is to be avoided by everyone. A thank you note can be written on a visiting card, business card, personal paper, or a small plain piece of paper on which to write your note. A man may write "Thank you" on the back of a correspondence card. A hand written note may be written on the front. **Get and use correspondence cards with matching envelopes and stamps.** You could use a blank 4 X 6 index card with an Invitation envelope. **Practice using them.** A man is to avoid using any fold-over card or indented correspondence card, or one with boarders. A woman may write a thank you note on a correspondence card. She could write "Thank you" on the front of a blank fold over card and a hand written note on the third page of the card. It might be written on the second and third page.

Practice writing mock thank you notes. You can send a copy to yourself.   **For a thank you note from you someone may wait for up to a year.**

Get back to a contact within 48 hours. Essentially, Re: Our Introduction "Nice meeting you," or "Thank you for the interview.

After an interview, whether or not you are interested in the position, follow-up with a "Thank you" letter. It is to be a note by hand. It can be in the form of an e-mail and should be sent immediately after the interview, and may be followed by the same note by hand.

Now home with you to write your Thank you notes, or at least the drafts; save a copy; do your business card reviews, and make notes in your log or journal, so that you have something to review prior to seeing the same people again.

Practice using personal and business cards. How else can you cultivate that wonderful memory and pretend that you are not keeping track?

Each note can contain a phrase about what was said at or what was enjoyed most about the event. You may say, "Thank you for the invitation to such a splendid event," or "Thank you for the such and such entertainment." You could say, "Many thanks for the excellent lunch yesterday. It was great catching up with you." Your card could include a phrase such as, "We will have to do it again real soon," "I know that it will not be long before we have "So and so" again. I'll call you in a few weeks to set a place and time," or "I look forward to the opportunity hearing from, and working for such an exceptional company."

In etiquette, two sentences can be a note. The host and/or hostess will know that you know that the next time it is your time to pay for the event and/or the entertainment.

The line to reciprocity is to ultimately lead to the meeting line located wherever you choose to hold your own activity. Your thank you might be said by a telephone call the next day or very soon after the event, but to whom can the receiver show your thank you call?

Avoid using e-mail for a thank you note, a love note, or to extend an expression of sympathy, when you can. When you do, you may send a follow-up note: the same note written by hand.

Special Ways to Say Thank You. When you were the guest of honor,

1. You can send flowers with a card to say, "Thank you" and that you, "Had a wonderful time." "So and so and I enjoyed ourselves at dinner last night" and "We both thank you very much." When an event was a joint guest-spouse one, the note is to be written, and any present sent, by the spouse.

2. When you are paying for meal, in a commercial dining room, you can say thank you to a server verbally and by leaving a tip. Be careful about eating in places where tipping seems to be mandatory (coffee shops,) prohibited, or optional. When you advance to eating in upscale dining rooms, the servers will not understand. Here, the server is taxed on a percent of your bill. It can cost her or him to serve you.

The tip is to be minimum 15% of the total bill minus tax. An increased tip can be provided for exceptional service. When a host says, "I got that." The reply is to be, "Thank you." (This is the first half of the first half.) The response here spoken or unspoken can be please "Come again."

Saying Thank You by Reciprocity

Part b. of the second half of saying "Thank you" is reciprocity. The rule of reciprocity – is to reciprocate "In kind:" When required. A guest is to extend an invitation -in kind to a host or hostess to reciprocate for any event or entertainment for which he or she attended where payment or work was not a requisite.

Mitigate the obligation: only accept invitations for the type of event or entertainment you are willing to give and from people you would like to invite to it (or work or pay a lot.)

The rule or reciprocity is **excepted when you** accept an invitation to an event where you have or had to **pay to attend.** Such events are a fundraiser, wedding shower, wedding, dance, or a ball.

It can be excepted **when you cannot reciprocate and that fact was known when the invitation was extended, and when** you are male, single, or are young. Enjoy and avoid pushing the three latter rules.

In public life, the rule of reciprocity could be omitted when the event was an expense account (work) lunch. However, a dinner is to be reciprocated-in kind, and normally in mixed pairs, or the excuse you offer had best be a good one.

Once someone acknowledges the requirement, at the activity, a senior guest can say, "Can I" or "Let me," and waive it, unless (you) the host insists.

Note: Unless you had to pay or work to attend an event, you are to reciprocate hospitality to a host before you entertain with anyone met at that event. You can include any newly met someone in your act of reciprocity.

Practice having reciprocal events: events in kind. People are to be invited to a like event to share drink atmosphere food and honor. Learn about precedence and seating assignments. It all goes with reciprocity. For reciprocity (even when required) a man can wait a lifetime.

When required reciprocity is to be done in rounds
- **Invitation:** respond to invitations within twenty-four hours to one week of receipt.
- **Acceptance:** you can accept the kind invitation…. Alert a host or hostess of meal restrictions along with your acceptance. Take note of the dress code or ask questions pertaining to it. Later, avoid being a no show, if possible.
- **Reciprocity:** for tips on handling reciprocity, you can review Flawless Dining Service.
- **Enjoy your new circle.**

Job Interview Tip:

For a job interview reciprocity can be a letter telling them that you are interested in the job. After a job offer, it can be a letter of acceptance saying, "Yes, I accept your kind offer." The rest is all about reciprocity.

Regrets

You can regret that you cannot accept the very kind invitation ….. The word "very" is the difference between acceptance and regret.

Questions

Business Dining Etiquette is about knowing all of this, practicing, and then pretending that "It just does not matter."

Congratulations on your upcoming graduation. Neat to see you will have some university dining etiquette lessons to go with that degree:

You will know your ascension has begun, when someone said to you more than once, "Let's do lunch."

Enjoy your climb. Remember to buy Forever stamps.

Know business dining etiquette, what is being signaled and what to signal back. Be aware of how you look when you eat, it is practical, civil, and the right thing to do.

Practice your lessons; enjoy your education. You can review these pages prior to coming to table.

Seating Assignments

The First Seat   the Seat of Honor at Table

Each seat at a table has a number assigned to it in precedence order. At a dinner, **the first seat to be assigned at a table is the seat of honor.** It is to allow a person in it to see the main entrance door, kitchen door, and the center and far backside of the room. It can allow the person in it to have his or her back to a wall in the room in which the event will be held. This seat is the head of the table.

1. **A host/ hostess or escort is to be assigned to each table.
   As a rule of thumb, the host** (HT) **is to get the first seat.** When the hostess (HTS) is to serve the meal her back is to be to the kitchen door depending on the room. Guests at a table are honored by their seating assignment.

2. In a commercial dining room, the first seat of honor is where to place the official host. Socially it can be where to place the person held in the highest esteem at an event: man number one (M1,) or woman number one (W1.) It is where to place a date. In business, this can be where to place the most senior person, the person holding the highest official rank (unless waived,) or where to place the guest of honor.

To do this, the host or hostess can move one place to the left from the seat of honor when that guest is of the opposite sex. He or she may move across from the seat of honor when the person is of the same sex or a senior person. This is done to give high honor to a guest. In a private home, the seat at the head of the table is for the host. He can relinquish this seat only to honor a head of state, or (when alone) a date.

There are rules for seating the Ex(tra) W Non Spouse

There are rules for Seating Singles w/ Couples

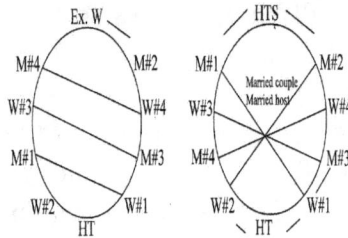

There are rules for Seating Non Multiple of Four.

A table is to be set at a number non-divisible by four (1, 6, or 10.) It can allow for the best show of married couple pairing: opposite and across, and honor at table.

There are rules for seating   There are rules for
the Ex(tra) W Non Spouse   Seating Singles w/ Couples

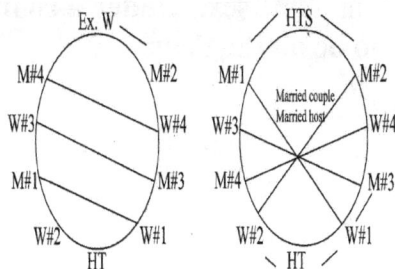

There are rules for Seating Same Sex Tables Right then left

There are booth rules- Men outside Women opposite across

There is a separate set of rules
For Honor at Table for Seating a Multiple of Four

At a table divisible by four if mixed pairing or separation of sexes is wanted, (at a stand-alone table) and it is, the person seated opposite the host is moved one place to the right with man number one. The person(s) that occupied the space(s) to the left of this person is/are moved down in honor order until the mixed pairs sequence is accomplished.

The person that cannot be mixed paired is moved clockwise to the next guest space of the same sex. **Under a roof – once seated at a table feet on are to be on the floor.**

The Cast at a Dining Event

At a dining event the cast can be as follows:

1. The Valet: the person who will park your car. If you let this happen, tip this person (one dollar-five dollars and the posted rate) on the way out.

2. The Maitre d' hotel: the person who will seat you (and handle any special request.) Tip this person (five to twenty dollars) on the way out after your rehearsal visit. Do this again periodically. For and from these people you can learn the art of palming money.

3. The Table Captain: the person who will take your order. The Server: the person who will serve you your meal. Tip the Captain five percent of the food bill minus tax. Tip the server fifteen- percent- minus tax. These two people can be one and the same.

4. The Wine steward (Sommelier :) the person who will present and pour your wine. Tip this person fifteen percent of the cost of the wine if service was provided, and occasionally he or she can be given what is left in the bottle of wine.

5.   The Bus person: the person who will pour your water, provide rolls (sliced bread) and butter, and clear your plates. (At banquets, sometimes this person will get something for you and is slipped a tip.)

6.   The Cashier: the person who will accept your credit card number in advance and/or your payment on the way to the bathroom. Say, "Thank you."

7.   The Owner: the person who has a good heart, a fragile ego, and a business to run. Tell this person, "It was wonderful." The Chef: the person who prepares your food, to whom you may send your compliments, and who earns your patronage. These people are not to be tipped.

8.   The Guest: the person who accepts the invitation, writes you a thank you note, and knows it will be his or her turn next time.

9.   The Event Host: the person who issued the invitation and who is to be allowed to "Take care" of the check: the person to whom is owed a thank you note and reciprocity.

Things to Avoid

While eating in company, there are things you want to avoid. Here are some of them.

1. In cocktail service, avoid using a napkin to wrap around your glass or drinking from a stirrer.

2. At table, avoid sitting down or picking up your napkin until the senior person does so, or touching your food until you receive a signal to dig in.

3. During the meal, avoid wrapping your arm around your plate, eating with your elbows on the table, talking with your mouth too full, slurping, being picky, placing a whole spoon bowl in your mouth, leaving your spoon in your soup bowl or cup when the course is finished, pouring sauce from a sauce boat, using a knife as you would use a saw, placing the knife and fork like a pair of oars, looking like a duck: leaning over your plate each time you take in food, smacking your lips, ignoring your meal partners, wiping your mouth with a napkin in one hand, while holding a spoon, knife, or fork in the other, gesticulating with a fork or knife.

Avoid taking your time, sharing meals" in business, " or asking to, eating everything on your plate, not knowing the company song, not dancing, asking to take any food home with you, placing the napkin on your plate, or in your glass, stacking plates or handing them to any serving staff, pushing a plate away from you (when you are finished,) leaning back in your chair, chewing gum anytime, leaving the table before you are excused, staying in the room when someone says, "We need to take a five to ten minute break," and

4.   Taking this all too seriously. (Trust me.)

Things to Avoid II --Avoid sharing information,

1.   When on a diet. Learn to say, "I would rather have (something else specific) please." When that something else comes, take it. Say, "Thank you."

2.   You can say, "I cannot. Doctor's orders," "Orders from the job," or "I need to lose ten pounds. I need you to help me."

3.   You may say, "I do not need to eat. I am allergic to it. It makes me break out in fat." On second thought, only you will think that that was funny. Enjoy your eating in company.

Eating in Company

In home training, first there was scrambling to the table, afterwards, each person received Eating "in company" instructions; they were

1.   "Do not touch your food until we are done saying grace." "Do not eat with your elbows on the table." "Do not talk with your mouth full." "Do not sing." And "Do not dance in your chair." Then there was, "Take your time." "Eat every bite; it's good for you." And "Do not leave the table until you are excused."

2.   Someone always asked, "Was not dinner good?" The reply was always, "I missed the TV."

In business dining etiquette, after seating people at the table what no one will tell you is there are eating-in-company instructions. They are adjuncts to and opposites of rules taught in home training.

1.   What someone will say is, "Ladies and gentlemen, please enjoy your dinner." Then, ("Elbows on the table are OK between courses.") ("Talk with some food in your mouth; keep your dinner partners company.") "Sing the company song." And "Dancing will be later on." Keep pace or you will hear, "For those of you still eating please continue, while we go on with the program." ("Gee, leave a little food on your plate.") And "(Get up,) we need to take a five to ten minute break."

2.   Someone will ask, "Was not dinner good?" The spoken reply will be, "Absolutely." (The unspoken reply will be, "I am still hungry.")

In between home training and business dinner there comes a time for university dining etiquette skills training: table manners "rules of etiquette used while eating," to transcend cafeteria behaviors and coffee shop ways.

When You Get Someone

When you get someone, there will come a time for new home training; you will encounter a meal called, "What is this ###?" It will be your favorite person, who contacted a contact, and now is trying to serve you your "Favorite dish." It will be followed by a meal called, "Some more." It is what you will ask for the next time that person tries to make you the same dish.

You can encounter a meal called, "Lets Share." Someone will say, "Try some of this." You will get to sample some of the meal that you ordered for someone else, and someone else will get to share some of a meal that was yours. When someone wishes to share food with you, provide the giver with a clean fork for the transfer. You can pass your plate to the giver with the attending implements in the finished position and have the portion placed directly onto your plate.

You will encounter a second helping called, "You eat the rest of this" and get to see someone scrape onto your plate food that no one else wants to eat. If you allow this, life will go on. There is a flip side to this, you will learn to say "You gonna eat that?" In addition, you could hear about Doggie bags.

In business dining, avoid asking for or accepting seconds and/or for Doggie bags, and all other of the above practices. They are separate and apart from University Etiquette Business Dining Casual and Fine Business Dining. They are things done among families and/or with people you would like to be in your family.

That "What is this ###?" meal can very well become the signature meal you take to an office potluck or serve when entertaining people at your in-home dinner party.

At home, eat some of everything that is served. Eat seconds whenever you can. Have a special meal that you like. Have some idea of what you want for each mealtime. Go to great lengths always to be on time. Be respectfully hungry. Do not talk with food in your mouth. Eat the kind of food eaten by the person with whom you want to sleep.

Eating is the most intimate thing you do with someone. This is not just a phrase. You can have a headache for a month. Never be, "Not hungry" for more than three days. Eating with someone can also be the most fun.

Good news. Practice can be done in casual shoes.

Notes
<u>Thoughts While You Were Eating</u> **by Harold Almon**
Educated eating is not to take a beating at a university: 9 units in living skills are to accompany each degree: learn the civil side of business administration.

One dining facility in which you eat is to have real plates, knives, forks, spoons, glasses, coffee cups, saucers and napkins. Students need the practice of establishing and maintaining a cover: (A Place Setting for One.)

If students are to overcome informal United States of America Café ways they must have exposure to better equipped cafeterias, and formal dining rooms.

Students need the practice of establishing a cover; a place setting for one, and hosting dining parties as if they could become one.

"My degree for a cup," once I graduate, someone will want to take me to lunch. There the person will see I have little practice using one.

How are you going to attract an interviewer or a date if all you make are garbage plates? When finished napkin on the side.

If you do not add class where you eat what you get to be is a clod with a degree. Change that. Polish gently.

You can get someone to make almost anything you want to eat as long as you are specific.

If you avoid being specific about what you want to eat, the person who would make it for you has no specific reason to get out of bed, just ask any child under twenty.

"I thought she thought I was a God. The first meal she served me was a burnt offering." Rick S&J July.

If you omit the time for sharing ambiance, and concentrate on just the intake of food, a good cook can kill you with consideration, one scoop for them, two scoops, and (later) the "rest of this," for you; take it and make it for lunch tomorrow.

If you omit eating a second helping at home, and do so somewhere else with your partner present, you will eat the next second helping at home.

Four Rules of Food: 1) it is to be universally available, 2) come from the food groups, 3) require behavior modification, (in proportion to intake,) and 4) you must be able to eat it for the rest of your life, or put it back, (unless it's for a celebration.)

A tray made for someone else requires a placemat. That's why that paper at Micky Ds and no mats at a cafeteria or buffet. (Etiquette) is everywhere.

While you were drinking from that opened can, a thought, what a place for a straw, and then from a cup w/o a lid, - a straw? Go figure.

"Happy Birthday to you, Happy Birthday to you, I've seen your table manners. You live in a zoo." – Joan Rivers during her shift at Denny's.

The difference between a gourmet and a gourmand: one is two steps above a glutton. The other is two steps above a garbage disposal.

"Eating with the most polished of manners is not a particularly attractive sight" – with dining etiquette skills training, this act can be transformed into a sight that is pretty and neat. This guide/class can help. I have seen you eat.

Teach him something, at an interview, or on a date, look at the person with you, not at the plate. Avoid making your feeding the reason for the meeting. Spend your whole life being book smart, gym fit, and napkin literate. You can outclass the competition.

Read Business Dining Guide 101 Job Preparation Four Pack Interview Dining Etiquette Eating in Style.   If I am eating with you and cannot tell that you have a degree, something is wrong. Read on gently.

Confidence and enthusiasm will not stop your eating poorly.

All the while you are eating someone will be signaling to you. He or she will be telling you what is known about table service, specific eating styles, rules concerning table manners at his or her table, and actions deemed acceptable, and someone will be waiting to see what you signal back. Be aware of how you look when you eat.

It is not fair, polite, or right to take a picture of your plate when you are in sight. Click. Go back and look at the picture I got – Take a picture too, for you, just for the fun of it.

Eti - Q Test Business Dining Etiquette Guide
Things to Learn and Do **Get Etiquette** Outclass the Competition

In addition to, the universal rule for eating in company,
"_____before leaving home"
1. Be punctual, _____, whatever this means in
your community. (Occasionally show up with a present.)
2.   N/A   Know where to wear that name badge
_____.
3.   N/A   Shake hands the right way_____.
4.   N/A   Do introductions (correctly,
_____then _____ or _____to
_____
5.   N/A   Mingle. Be good company. When
someone gives you a business card, know what to do with it
_____, and what to have to give
back. _____.
6.   N/A   Know how to respond to an offer of a drink,
during daylight. Order _____. It is easier to say than
_____.
7.   N/A   Learn how to survive a business party: how to
hold a napkin, glass, and a plate, in your _____,
functionally.
8. Drink without poking someone in the eye; avoid the crane;
raising your elbow to take a drink from a glass.)
_____. _____ liquid into your
mouth, from your wrist. Do this _____. When not
drinking, _____ (And wash
your hands before you come to or stay at the table.)

9. Know the standard USA menu number and order of courses:
_____, _____, _____, _____, _____, _____.
Learn what to do after reading that reusable menu_____.
10.   Maintain your cover: _____, or establish one.
11.   N/A   Know which fork to use: name six,
_____, _____, _____, _____, _____, _____, and when.
12. Avoid bread until _____; remember bread is not a first course. Avoid leaving _____ in bread that you are eating.
13. Talk. At a family dinner, know an invocation acceptable to your host's culture._____. Keep the people at your table company. (Remember, for some, your conversation is the entertainment.) Talk about things other than work (unless it is the purpose for the meal.) Use your inside voice. Some _____ can still be in your mouth. Know what to do when someone stops to visit you at table. _____.
14. When seated at a table, place a napkin _____ before eating or drinking anything.
15. Look for food to be served (counter-clockwise) from _____ (leaving.) At a table -- look for drinks at table to be served from _____ (refreshing)
Know the menu order of courses for the day _____, _____, _____, and _____.Order something easy: that you know how to eat. Eat in _____ over eating in piles.) Avoid taking too little, or too much, or more in visual calories than those dining around you.
Try a little of everything unless restricted by religion, health, or culture.

16. Eat each meal in an accepted style: _____ or
_____. _____ in only one
direction, one _____ at a time. (Yes, you may
eat only one thing at a time.) **Keep your hands on the table.** Sit up
straight. _____.) Close your mouth
around the edge of any fork placed in it. Chew each portion
_____, with your mouth closed, and saver each
bite. Taste buds live and digestion begins _____
not the stomach yes that's right. Make as _____
as possible.

17. Pace yourself. Eat each course in such a manner as to finish
it_____. Avoid eating too little, too much, or too
fast, or acting as if the meal is to be your last. When at a loss as to
how to eat a particular dish_____ You can ask
_____?" The lesson most likely will begin
with a smile. Take _____ often. Rest the
_____ on the edge of the table. You can rest your
elbows on the table _____. (Continentally, you
can talk with a knife and fork in your hands._____.
Learn the rules for water, Bread, and how to eat chicken with a
knife and fork.

18. **Avoid adding** salt or pepper to food, unless it is to _____,
_____, _____, _____, or _____. When
salt is requested, ensure _____ Avoid _____.

19. Before temporarily leaving a table, place flatware in
_____ for the style in which you are eating. Get
up; place your napkin _____. Know what to do when
someone visits your table_____. Between courses,
_____. **Visit Station Six.**

20. At table finishes. Before permanently leaving a table, place flatware in _____ for the style in which you are eating. In public, _____ of each course on your plate and of each drink in each glass. Leave each course plate _____until it is removed by a waitperson or replaced by the next plate. Look for food to be removed from _____ (retrieving.)

21. Place your napkin in a mock fold to the_____ (leaving) side of your place setting, (again napkin on the side.)   A napkin is to be crisp at the end When its time, sing the company song_____. When it is time, dance. Let the host pay (and tip) where required. OK back to class.

22.   Remember reciprocity, where required. Read and research as   much   as   possible   the   culture   in   which   you _____.

Watch each act of eating with an open mind, eye, and heart. Practice diligently. While eating in company, there are things to learn and do. – This is the short course _____For answers read the blog, read the book, or bring this test to class. N/A items are from the next class.

I know you want - Manners in a minute – done – but just some. Maths took months, but to get etiquette; it takes practice, that's the rest of life's test.

Breakfast

A boiled egg is to be eaten by using an eggcup, an underlying plate set in a place setting, and a teaspoon.

1. The cup is steadied with the left hand. The teaspoon is used to tap or to crack the top of the shell (same as with crème Brulee.)

2. The top shell is removed and placed on the underlying plate.

3. The egg is to be eaten by being spooned from the shell and placed into the mouth. Yes, you can add salt to a boiled egg without first tasting it.

4. The finished position for the spoon is to the right side of the eggcup atop the underlying plate.

Bacon is to be eaten by using a knife and fork to cut it and using a fork to place it in the mouth. It can be rolled with knife onto a fork, prior to being taken into the mouth. Bacon that is very crisp can be picked up and taken to the mouth using the fingers.

When cereal is to be eaten, a cereal bowl and an underlying plate are to be placed center the place setting. A bread and butter plate is to be used as an underlying plate. A salad plate can be used. It may be a dinner plate. (Only a salad bowl can be correctly placed directly on a table.)

1.   Cereal is eaten using a spoon.

2.   The rest position for the spoon is center the bowl handle pointed to four o'clock.

3.   The bowl can be tipped away from the table to get the last bit of cereal or milk from within it.

4.   The finished position for the bowl is center the setting atop an underlying plate.

5.   The finished position for the spoon is to the right side of the bowl on the underlying plate.

6.   Avoid eating cereal as the last course to any meal except breakfast. If you are "still hungry" eat some fruit, something someone watching can understand. Cereal may be eaten later, when you are alone, as a snack. Avoid someone watching you practice being too poor to have proper seconds.

Fast Food Etiquette

In fast food service tray service, a sandwich, fries, and drink or the equivalent is to be served on a tray. A tray made for someone else is to be covered with a placemat. This was a rule long before the advent of anything named "Mickey D's," or the breach by "Bell."

1. An additional placemat is to be requested for each person to be at the table. Each person is to be provided with a placemat. (Ask for the extras and glasses for water – even if you have to buy them.) Get napkins, and optionally real knives and forks.

2. The tray is to be carried to the table. Remember to select a seat to show honor to the person with you. Give up the seat to which the person with you will gravitate – the seat of honor.

3. Food given in a bucket or box is to be placed to the left of each person who is to receive one. Glasses are to the set above the place setting space. Placemats are to be provided. Then using a wrapper or a plate, as a base, items are to be set on a placemat in cover: in a place setting configuration.

The tray is to be taken to the stand for it. Sit down. Looks like it cost more already. Eat and Be at Ease.

A Fast Food Cover

A plate is to be provided or a wrapper is to be used as one, and a cover: a place setting for one is to be established. Each food item is to be taken out of each container, and set in a place setting for one, a cover, one item at a time. The napkin is to be placed to the left of the place setting, initially. When eating alone, the beverage item(s) can be placed on the table above the space for it. Then the placemat and contents on it can be slid onto the table, and adjustments made to any item requiring it. The beverage item(s) may then be placed to the right top of the main plate, and the tray taken to the tray stand.

(In a family setting, a host is responsible for the invocation and for controlling table talk.) The napkin is picked up at the lead of the senior person, and placed on the lap. At a business meeting or dinner party an invocation is to be omitted. It can be done. It may not be according to etiquette.

Avoid eating out of a bucket, box, or a bag. You have already paid for the food. You deserve a plate (wrapper) or a dish, and a knife, fork, and a spoon, and optionally a glass. "Fast" is to refer just to the food delivery. Once you sit at a table, a wrapper becomes a plate. You can unfold it and eat the item as if from a dish. A Wrap, Burrito, or a Burger in a Wrapper can be a whole meal in a hand; each is better suited to a standing working man.

A large sandwich is to be placed to the bottom third of the plate or wrapper. It can be cut in half. A non-grilled sandwich may be lifted with the fingers brought to the mouth, and a manageable piece bitten off, and eaten. Drain   salsa   before adding it to a Burrito or when you pick it up it will drip.

Avoid the duck and chuck: dipping your head down to meet food coming to you. Sit up with your back straight and your neck up. A sandwich with a sauce, grilled or a hot open-faced, is to be eaten using a fork and knife: albeit, each may be made of plastic.

Packets containing condiments may be provided. The top of the condiment holder can be torn off, the condiment squeezed onto the plate, and the top placed into the bottom of the holder, and then placed to the left side of the plate. In service that is more formal, such packets are omitted. Get a napkin. The vendor can afford them. Whatever is lost on condiments is made up on napkins.

French fries can be removed from the container they were served in and placed to the right of the sandwich on the plate or wrapper. The package they came in may be folded up and placed to the left of the place setting space. Fries can be eaten with a fork. They may be cut in half using the side of it. The fork could be used to impale each fry and to incorporate catsup on it as it is taken to the mouth.

The package could be used as a side cup. Fries might be eaten with fingers.

Trick question; when is a bag not a plate? Answer; when you are in a place where you can ask for a plate.

When handed dinner in a bag, box, or container it is to be used to carry food to the table, with or without a tray. A bag can be emptied, folded flat, and used to set food atop, in absence of a wrapper or a plate. Contents from a bag can be eaten from atop one, or placed onto a wrapper or a plate. A wrapper can be placed atop a folded bag, and used as a plate. It can be set to the left of the plate space to be discarded, when proved a plate. Containers are to be used to help serve food to a bag, plate (wrapper,) or bowl.

For each item you are to establish a cover: a place setting for one.

Avoid feeding from within a bag. A feed bag is for a horse. (Eat, from one, and next someone will be handing you cubes of sugar.)

Fast Food Drinking

1. When doing Fast Food drinking avoid drinking out of a
    container, when you can. You can order the value size soda.
    The refills are generally free. Under a roof, if you get a
    drink that you have to drink with a straw, to get to the
    bottom of your glass, perhaps you are drinking from a
    pitcher, or at best a carafe, ask for a value size or water
    glass to go with that.

2. Under a roof, ask for a glass or a cup "for here". Each can be
    requested and used to receive any beverage provided in a
    container: a can, bottle, carton, or thermos. When under a
    roof, at a minimum, if your drink has a lid on it and you can
    take it off. If a container has a twist of top, or has to be
    opened up; get a cup, a glass, or a straw. Remember when
    the half-pint milk carton came with a straw and a thermos
    came with a cup? The rule remains; the behavior changed.

3. You can carry a cup with you in a backpack or briefcase for
    drinks served in a container. You may ask for a cup "For
    here." You may ask for a straw, if your beverage is in a
    container, a straw can be used to drink it. Under a roof, you
    could omit the lid.

4.   Avoid containers and straws when you can. Avoid drinking on the go? Gotta – I know. Get a container and a straw. Grab a napkin to 'Go with' that – just a better class of drinking. The napkin is to be held between the middle and the ring finger. Avoid wrapping the napkin around as a sleeve.

Outside, at a table, when a drink is served in a glass or cup without a lid, the straw is optional, but unless you are a romantic or a big kid, it is to be overcome. Avoid using a glass and a straw in a dining room. A napkin is to be placed on the lap prior to drinking or eat at a table.

Under a roof, get, "A cup for here." Get a "To go" cup if you must. The lid is to be removed and placed to the left of the place setting. Even when the beverage is hot, at some point you are too big for a Sippy glass.

A large cup to go is to be filled no more than half full. Avoid having over 16 ounces of liquid taken up to your lips as you take a sip. A 32 ounce container of liquid was once labeled "Family size." Imagine what someone could think of you had the beverage been wine. This container may be used to fill a cup for here.

5.   The cup is to be picked up in the right hand, and from the base, the beverage taken and sipped or poured into the mouth from the hand from the wrist. You can always refill it, once. You can refill your container again, just before you go.

About refills, when you are going to get one you can say, "Can I get anything for you?" (The trip is priceless. The liquid is free.)

You can always top it off, before you are really ready to leave, or not. It is a cup "to go." You may avoid doing any of this and dine at places which provide a cup "for here."

Away from a table, a lid with a hole in it may be used to drink a beverage from a cup with or without a straw. Each could minimize the effect should the cup be jarred. This is ideally suited for babies, computer operators, and for astronauts. This might also be done when a person is drinking in a car or where allowed on a bus.

Note: I see you have practice drinking with a straw. What I am not sure of is if you can drink without one. Under a roof, avoid drinking with a straw whenever possible.

Fast Food Finishes

In a fast food restaurant, when a course is finished,

1.   A cupped palm over a plate can indicate, "Please remove this." A cupped palm over a heart may be used to say, "(No) Thanks." The plate or container could be moved to the right of the place setting or to the outer edge of the table. (You may pretend as if you really expected a waitperson to remove it.)

2.   This is to be done to allow a place for the next course cafeteria or box style. Courses are to be eaten one at a time. The plate can be moved to the right and cleared once the next plate is served. Dessert anyone?

3.   The plate or container for the last course is to be left in place center the place setting (in a finished position not a trashed one.) "To go" containers are to be placed into a bag; "Yes (you would like one,) paper." "Thank you." The placemat can be moved to the side of the table so the "Work" you brought to do may now be done.

4.   The napkin is to be placed to the left of the place setting; be able to take a picture. Better to take the napkin with you than to leave it center a dirty plate. (OK, now pretend that someone wanted to give you a fabric napkin; leave it to the left.)

5.   When a fast food waitperson is to bus your table; leave this person a tip of about 3-5 percent of the cost of the meal. A tip is to be at least two quarters left on the table (where allowed.)

Note: there can be a place for that roll in cart, or a need to hire someone to bus that table, and sometimes for someone to be your server, to "Bring that right out to you."

Bussing your Table

Bussing your own table can be more the custom of a fast food environment and may be more in line with the wishes of your dinner companion. Push in your chair until it is six inches away from the table. Reset the salt and pepper holders.

Reestablish the "Centerpiece."   Kidding, no touching the centerpiece.

Yes I really believe you can bus your cover.

1.   Place the beverage container above the place setting.

2.   Pick up the left edge of the placemat in the left hand between the thumb and the index finger.

3.   Balance disposable utensils on the wrapper or plate and grasp the plate or wrapper by the thumb of the left hand.

4.   Fold the placemat backward over or under the plate or wrapper and grasp it.

5.   Use your napkin to crumb the table. Then place the napkin under the placemat along with any trash or empty packet(s.)

6.   Grasp each piece with the fingers of the left hand.

7.   Next, pick up the beverage container(s) in the right hand.

You can carry the container or glass on the palm of the left hand. Avoid stacking a container or glass on a plate.

8.   Take the trash to the trash receptacle and deposit it. In other dining rooms, maintain the look of a plate that could accept seconds until you get to the plate rack or garbage can. You can omit bussing the table in favor of leaving a tip. Carry cash for this act, just in case you cannot add a tip to a tab paid with a card.

When in company, a host or hostess may bus the table: it could be done with a retrieved tray.

1.   The napkins are to be placed to the left of the center on the tray. Trash can be placed to the left of the napkins.

2.   Plates may be stacked on top of each other, center the tray. (I cannot believe that I have said that.)

3.   Utensils and glasses could be placed to the right of the tray. Then the tray might be taken to the designated location and emptied, and placed on the space provided for it.

In fast food service, you will be thought of fondly if you will, carry a tray, set each place setting, or help to clear a table. In rooms that are more formal, the latter practice is to be omitted. Bottom line; avoid making dirty trays or garbage plates.

Next, you can

Practice Cafeteria and Buffet Style Service. Be at ease.

1. After you pay or sign in, for your meal, get a table a chair, and then when eating in courses, get a plate for bread. Bread is to be present at a table when eating in company. You can be the bread person. Get a plate or basket of rolls or buns for everyone, plus one or two just to view, and bread and butter plates, (and get butter too if you can find some.)

2. Remember to establish a cover. Avoid taking a fork to table alone – even here when you can pair it with a knife. A glass for water is required when eating in company. It can be for wine where water is scarce. A second glass can be used to hold what you drink as "wine." No drinking on the way to the table.

3. After establishing a cover, avoid approaching the food table too fast.

4. Avoid putting too much food onto your plate, filling two plates at the same time, looking like you are trying to serve your whole table, or looking as you are eating for the last time. Eat in courses over eating in piles.

5. Leave your used plate center the place setting. Leave silver at the table in the finished position, before helping yourself to the next selection. Each course is to get its own set of flatware.

Flatware can be set in a rest position, on a plate, (when only one set is provided; I only mention this because it happens.

Get the next course. Then you can take the finished plate to the bussing station or push the plate up or to the side for someone to take. It may have already been taken. (Let dreams live.) Avoid pushing or passing trash. Except at breakfast, avoid eating cereal as your last course or dish. This, again, is something I have witnessed.

What makes this frugal? Once you have paid you can stay and eat until the end of the dining period. You can invite a date, and know exactly what it is going to cost you. You can still tip like a player, where appropriate.

Now back to home and eating alone. You may practice eating frozen dinners or meals on wheels, both are just other forms of pre-paid meal plans.

1. Contents of each reheated dish are to be covered with a plate and turned onto it or spooned out onto one, and a cover is to be established before the meal is eaten.

2. You owe yourself napkin and a glass, a plate or a dish, and optionally a knife and a fork.

3. You can do the same with items that are delivered. Now that you have "cooked," you may invite someone to join you for table talk.

Eating in the Chinese or Japanese Style

1. Food can be cut before the time it is cooked.

2. It is to be eaten primarily with chopsticks. The first chopstick is placed horizontally at the base of the index finger and at the front knuckle of the ring finger. It is supported by the middle finger of a bent hand. The chopstick pair is to be held with the thumb and the index finger.

3. Chopsticks are to be held near the top centered and parallel to each other. They are used as pinchers or as two grasping jaws to pick up the food item desired.

4. A bowl placed in front of each person, at a cover, is to be picked up in the left hand and eaten from with the right hand.

5. Rice is to be eaten in between eating each dish even when switching back to the dish. Food taken from a bowl, dish, or platter is to be secured and balanced. Then it is bought to or over the plate of the person intended to receive it, even if only in mock form prior to the time the wrist is turned in and upwards and the food is taken to the mouth.

6.   Chopsticks remain in the right hand throughout the meal unless placed in the rest or finished position for them.

7.   When chopsticks are placed in the rest position they are to be collapsed by being brought together with the thumb and the index finger side by side and placed onto a chopstick rest, a plate, or across a bowl.

8.   Avoid placing chopstick standing up in any bowl or dish. The finished position for chopsticks is placed diagonally across the center of the plate pointed to four o'clock. They can be placed parallel to the edge of the table.

9.   Chopsticks are to be used in sharing table manners in an Asian environment, when appropriate. You can practice with popcorn. Pickles when served are to be eaten last.

Note: Chinese chopsticks have square tips, Japanese chopsticks have rounded tips.

Note: In Asian and other countries.   You can dine in some restaurants only by invitation or introduction.

Learn how to drink tea in ceremony.

1. The tea period is used to determine who you are and where you fit into your company's pecking order.

2. It can be used to determine how your status relates to your host's status. Information about you will be passed among those present as well as to people not in the room.

3. From this ceremony, determination will be made on how precisely to deal with you.

Enjoy your review.

Considerate Actions

When you accept an invitation to an event for which you do not have to pay to attend, perform considerate actions. You will be considered for sainthood:

1. When you are the guest of honor, you can send ahead a small arrangement of flowers to the hostess's office, or some cut flowers to her home or to the place at which the event will be held.

2. Remember to arrive on time whatever that may mean in your community.

3. When you are just a plain guest you can bring a present of a bottle of something to drink (wine where alcohol is welcome), or a non-alcoholic drink to give to the hostess. It may be opened at the event.

4. Know how to wear a name tag. Know the rules for wearing your own and for wearing one that is provided. Take a head shot. The name badge is to be within the frame. Be prepared to give and to receive a visiting card. Ideally, have a business or organizational visiting card. Write down the names of the people with whom you spoke: people who served you, and the name and address to use when sending a note saying, "Thank you."

5.   Be prepared to share one to three humorous stories. Then do so, only if there is an extreme need. Keep your dinner partner company.

6.   Plan for and prepare a toast to the health, wealth, or well being of the honoree (or) event. You can ask permission to offer a toast when the dessert course is being served, when the host has yet to do so. When clicking glasses, to honor someone, click your glass rim lower than the other.

7.   Carry money for tipping, taxies, and emergencies. Carry a time piece (a pocket timepiece with black tie,) a pencil, and a pen.

8.   Carry a breath mint or a gum made with cinnamon. Perform small services: offer to open a window, find out the time, etc., when the desire for each is identified.

9.   At a home, with anyone considered family, or where minor children are at table, you do well to occasionally show up with a rose for the cook, or to extend an offer to do dishes.

10. Carry a handkerchief. You can carry a zip plastic bag and a paper napkin in a back pack or briefcase. Each is not for you but for her. Accidents happen. Be prepared for someone to say, "Thank you."

11. Know these things, share your presence and present, display business dining etiquette, get etiquette skills training, and then "Pretend that it just does not matter."

Business Dining Etiquette Guide 101 is done. You can review Business Dining Etiquette Guide 301 Look professional and polished. Reviewing listed skills can be essential prior to attending any business dinner. -- Education preparation and practice can help you outclass the competition.

You cannot know how to dance just because someone has invited you to a ball. But then again someone thinks highly of you and is sure that you can learn the steps with practice, you did get that invitation.

Business Dining Etiquette Guide 101   Harold Almon's

Some Harold Almon's Living Skills Etiquette Guides for Young Professionals and University Seniors can be ordered on Amazon.com, or Ebay.com. A full selection of Living Skills Etiquette Guides and product details can be previewed at Lulu.com Harold Almon and ordered there by direct request using Add to Cart. Excerpts can be read at: Be at Ease School of Etiquette blog: http://baeschoolofetiquette.blogspot.com/

Austin Food Inside Tours University Dining Club Lessons and University Etiquette Guide Lessons are available for each title.

www.ingramcontent.com/pod-product-compliance
Lightning Source LLC
Chambersburg PA
CBHW060509030426
42337CB00015B/1811